Esau's Blessing

How the Bible embraces those with Special Needs

Ora Horn Prouser

Teaneck, New Jersey

ESAU'S BLESSING ©2011 Ora Horn Prouser. All rights reserved. No part of this book may be used or reproduced in any manner whatsoever without written permission except in the case of brief quotations embodied in critical articles and reviews.

Published by Ben Yehuda Press
430 Kensington Road
Teaneck, NJ 07666

http://www.BenYehudaPress.com

Ben Yehuda Press books may be purchased for educational, business or sales promotional use. For information, please contact:
Special Markets, Ben Yehuda Press,
430 Kensington Road, Teaneck, NJ 07666
markets@BenYehudaPress.com

ISBN13 978-1-934730-35-5

Cover photo by Suzanne Tucker / shutterstock.com

Library of Congress Cataloging-in-Publication Data

Prouser, Ora Horn.
 Esau's blessing : special needs in the Bible / Ora Horn Prouser.
     p. cm.
 Includes bibliographical references.
 ISBN 978-1-934730-35-5
 1. People with disabilities in the Bible. 2. Bible. O.T.--Criticism, interpretation, etc. I. Title.
 BS1199.A25P76 2011
 221.8'3624--dc23
                          2011037309

    11 12 13 / 10 9 8 7 6 5 4 3 2   20111102

To Joe, Shira, Eitan, and Ayal
with profound love and deep appreciation

מִי שָׂם פֶּה לָאָדָם, אוֹ מִי-יָשׂוּם אִלֵּם, אוֹ חֵרֵשׁ אוֹ פִקֵּחַ אוֹ עִוֵּר—
הֲלֹא אָנֹכִי, ה'.

שמות ד:יא

Who places a mouth in human beings, or who is it that makes one mute or deaf or seeing or blind? Is it not I, God?

Exodus 4:11

I thank God for my handicaps, for, through them, I have found myself, my work, and my God.

Helen Keller

Contents

Acknowledgements

The process of writing a book takes a very long time, and this book is the product of many years of thinking and researching with several stops and starts along the way. I am indebted to many people who gave of their knowledge and support in many ways.

Eve and Larry Yudelson at Ben Yehuda Press believed in this manuscript and took the many steps necessary to bring it to publication with sensitivity and careful attention.

Everything we are as teachers and scholars is thanks to our teachers, our students, and our colleagues. Special thanks to Dr. Edward Greenstein who not only was one of my most important professors of Bible throughout my education and my dissertation advisor, but who remains a major influence in my life and work in so many ways. His support and encouragement from the very first moment that I told him about the kernel of this idea stayed with me throughout the writing of this book. I feel blessed to teach at The Academy for Jewish Religion, and am constantly enriched by the passion, devotion, and love of Torah of my students and colleagues at AJR. I have been lucky enough to teach parts of this book along the way in various classrooms and venues. The creative, and caring students in all of those classes enriched my thinking and my work in countless ways. Thanks also go to Dr. Steve Brown and Bette Birnbaum who helped with an earlier iteration of this manuscript.

Most importantly, I thank my family who has stood by me with tremendous encouragement in all of my work, and, particularly in support of this book. I am blessed to be a part of a large and involved family, and I know that I am better able to be the kind of person and professional that I want to be thanks to their support and love. I want to make special mention of my brother, my sister, their spouses, my cousins…. My parents, Rabbi Bill and Dena Horn, have been involved with and supportive of me in every way, and took special interest in this project. My husband, Rabbi Joseph Prouser, my emotional and intellectual partner, was always there with a helpful word, a useful reference, great editing skills, and a kind understanding that this was a long process. And, my children, Shira, Eitan, and Ayal, have taught me so much about life, and people, and have given me a greater appreciation of the beauty of variety than I could have learned in any book, lecture, or study. I could not have done this without you.

Preface

I have always felt great compassion for Esau. Having studied the Bible through the lens of traditional interpretation, I was accustomed to read Jacob as the wonderful son and Esau as the black sheep of the covenantal family. Later, I came to defend Esau, insisting on his good qualities without being sure why. I remember the day when it all clicked.

I attended a study session on Genesis in which the lecturer described Esau's impulsiveness: selling his birthright; eating; and leaving immediately thereafter. Around that same time I had been reading extensively about attention deficit hyperactivity disorder (ADHD). Upon hearing the lecturer's description of Esau, I leaned over to a companion and whispered with a chuckle that maybe Esau had ADHD. My own comment stuck in my mind and I began to rethink the text from a new perspective. Small details suddenly fit together in a more coherent way. (This insight will be addressed in more depth in Chapter 1.) Seen in this light, Esau no longer appeared an evil man with misplaced priorities, but rather, a portrait emerged of someone with learning issues who had never received the gift of being understood.

As the idea developed, I began to read other biblical characters through this lens. Initially, I focused on individuals who somehow did not seem to fit the mold. I soon realized that a number of biblical personalities could also be read as having special needs. Further, I came to believe that there was much to be gained from a compassionate reading of the text: It encourages seeing each character as having been created in the image of God, *b'tselem Elohim*. Such a reading invites us not to be so quick to dismiss those characters with challenges (in the text, and by extension, in our own lives), and gives us a greater opportunity to deepen our relationship with all of God's creation. Reading the text in this way also serves the function of enriching the conversation, biblical as well as educational, at a time when it is becoming clear that "normal" development, or behavior that we consider "typical," is a receding ideal!

Views differ as to the legitimacy of looking back at historical and literary characters to make modern diagnoses. The tools we would need to make these claims, such as school records and the like, are not available, so of course I do not lay claim to any authoritative portrayal of the characters' historical biographies. My primary concern is neither with the original intent of the text nor with the most probable meaning. Rather, my aim is to extend the meaning of a sacred text by looking through an inclusive lens that allows it to be read in a new way. For certain major characters who present with overt disabilities, like Moses, the information is clearly present in the text. With close reading, it can be seen that the Bible contains other characters who have special emotional, behavioral, or physical needs. There is much for us to learn from how these characters see themselves, how they are treated, and how they are addressed by God.

In the following chapters, I use an interpretive framework that is careful and deliberate to examine the text's nuances and unique literary devices within the realm of *peshat,* the contextual meaning. In other words, none of these readings argue against the details or structure of the biblical text. I strive throughout to find support for all elements of the interpretation through the language, themes, and style present in the text. I have taken care to build each case with multiple textual supports and have never based a conclusion on one or two verses alone. Given my great appreciation for and delight in the translation method of Dr. Everett Fox, many of the translations of biblical texts here draw extensively on his work in The Five Books of Moses. In addition, I have drawn on the translations of the New Jewish Publication Society Tanakh which are often elegant and smooth.

In this book, I have limited myself to educational issues only. The single chapter that stands outside this framework concerns depression. That was included because today there is a rising number of children who suffer from depression, both in school and in society at large, and this impacts on their learning. In addition, since depression can arise from undiagnosed or misunderstood learning disabilities, it has become an important issue for many education professionals. These parameters, however, have led me to exclude readings of other very interesting characters whose needs are outside the realm of education, such as King Saul.

As a biblicist who cares very deeply about the Bible, I have found through study and teaching that lessons from the Bible can be brought to bear on a very large range of contemporary issues. As Rabbi ben Bag Bag said, *hafokh bah, hafokh bah, dekulei bah.* "Pore over it again and again, for everything is in it" (Pirkei Avot 5:26). I do not know whether the ancient Rabbis conceived of the layers of meaning that modern readers would find in the biblical text. However, I am moved religiously and spiritually to find that the text of the Bible is so rich that it can even serve as a basis for discussing issues of special education.

This book shows that there is a valuable connection between the study of the Bible and the field of special education. Both fields benefit from the work. The conclusions of this study have biblical, educational, and religious implications. For those who read the Bible, this work provides new insights into biblical characters and the attitude of the Bible toward people with disabilities. It also creates a unique interpretive model that can be applied across the entire biblical text. For those in the field of special education, this book provides a framework that anchors their good work firmly in an ancient tradition and calls attention to its holy purpose.

I wrote this book as a professional Jewish educator. As a Jewish community, we are only beginning to address the needs of the differently abled, and much work remains to be done. I have observed children who are unable to receive an appropriate Jewish education, or who face constant struggles in trying to get their schools to understand and provide for their individual needs. Looking at our sacred text in this new way can provide spiritual support for those students, their families, and their teachers. God enfolds them in God's question for Moses, "Who makes [man] dumb or deaf, seeing or blind? Is it not I, the Lord?" (Exodus 4:11). Reading the text with these new connections can help us to imagine our special needs brethren in the embrace of a loving God, and instructs us to respond in a similar compassionate manner.

Tremendous religious and spiritual fulfillment flows from reading the Bible through the lens of special needs. I believe that the beauty and sacredness of the Bible increase exponentially as we apply more of its texts to aspects of our modern life. As we engage in this study of the text and its educational implications, we should keep in mind the reverent nature of this process. I hope that this study will add to the growing literature that expands the range of topics that can be addressed through the study of Bible. Each time we include a new discipline in our study of the Bible, we find another connection between our Scripture and ourselves.

That important biblical characters can be understood as having special needs provides further illustration that the Bible truly is for *all* people. Everyone, in one way or another, can find a place within the familiar biblical text. In addition, the presence of special needs in the Bible reinforces its value as a tool for teaching us how to conduct ourselves in the world. This book confirms that the Bible wants us to treat people with disabilities with dignity and respect.

This study also reconsiders some of the biblical characters that seem to have been drawn in a negative light. As we identify these figures' special needs, we can put their challenges into a more positive framework. The chapters on Esau and Isaac make this clear. When we appreciate the impact of special needs on the lives of individuals and their families (whether they are characters from the Bible or people we know), we stand a better chance of meeting them halfway.

It is my hope that this book can help us recognize the role that special needs play in our tradition, and encourage our religio-social mandate to do everything in our power to embrace and nurture people with special needs and their families.

Introduction

"Educating in God's Image"

Traditional texts from the Bible, Pirkei Avot, rabbinic writings and the Responsa literature have all addressed the realities of living with disabilities.[1] Attitudes about the disabled in these sources range from acceptance and understanding to rejection and exclusion. However, all of these texts recognize that the Israelite and, later, Jewish community[2] have always included people with special physical, emotional, and educational needs.

In the Bible, physical and mental disabilities have a negative impact on qualifications for priestly service.[3] At the same time, the Bible says that treating the deaf and blind with respect and protection is holy (*kadosh*) and God-fearing behavior (Leviticus 19:14). Proverbs exhorts us to "Train a lad in the way he ought to go" (22:6). One interpretation of this verse requires that we educate each child according to his or her style of learning,[4] a deep recognition that individuals respond to different educational approaches.

Bringing the matter of special needs into the study of the Bible should go beyond finding a few relevant texts to enliven the discus-

---

[1] Many have tried to address the needs of the disabled community. See, e.g., Rahamim Melamed-Cohen and Yoel Schwartz.

[2] I use the term *Israelite* to refer to the people before the time of the Babylonian Exile in the sixth century BCE. I use the term *Jewish* to refer to the people following the Exile, after they have become a people with an identifiable religion based on something other than their place of residence.

[3] See, e.g., Leviticus 21:16-24. For a fuller discussion of this issue, see Judith Z. Abrams, *Judaism and Disability*, and Thomas Hentrich, "Masculinity and Disability in the Hebrew Bible," 82-84.

[4] Schwartz, 58.

sion. Rather, disability studies can shed new light on our understanding of the Bible as a whole. The field of disability studies has become an important academic discipline within the humanities. Just as women's studies has added so much to the reading of the Bible, extending far beyond our understanding of individual women in the text, so too, disability studies has been making its way into biblical studies. "One of the goals of disability studies should be, then, to knit disability as a category of analysis into all of the courses in which we examine the workings of culture, especially courses that address issues of representation, identity, subjectivity, or the political implications of ideology."[5] Seeing the Biblical text in this way gives us not only a fresh perspective on the text, but also a new way of seeing the differently abled. Instead of seeing deficit, we can see others no less loved, yet perhaps more vulnerable than ourselves and in greater need of our sensitivity. In this way, the text points to the possibility of our own personal growth.[6]

On the surface, the cast of characters in biblical narrative texts includes individuals who experience emotional, physical, and behavioral challenges. This phenomenon is not unique to the Bible, since "images of disability have always been important in Western myth and literature."[7] However, it is common for pre-modern literature to stereotype people with disabilities. Some are characterized as villains, or as self-haters. Others are portrayed as pathetic recipients of the community's pity and charity. Often, they function to allow the community at large to feel good about itself as it cares for the less fortunate in its midst.[8]

---

[5] Thomson, 296.
[6] An excellent survey of the literature on disability studies within biblical studies can be found in Raphael, *Biblical Corpora*, 5-28.
[7] Fries, 4.
[8] Ibid.

Remarkably, such stereotypes do not typify the Hebrew Bible's portrayal of the disabled. In fact, characters with disabilities are among the most heroic personages in Scripture. Moses, one of the strongest and most positive biblical personalities, has a speech difficulty that never detracts from his stature. Similarly, Jonathan's son, Mephiboshet, who suffers from a physical disability, defies the categories of "villain" and "charity case." Mephiboshet benefits by eating at King David's table and receiving all of Saul's land as an inheritance. However, Mephiboshet later suffers from David's lack of awareness of his disability and the limitations thus imposed on his life. (Mephiboshet will be discussed more fully later in this volume.)

In bringing the field of disability studies to bear on biblical studies, I wish to emphasize that the Hebrew Bible does not fit the traditional mold because it does not depict the disabled as villains or outsiders. Rather, these personalities are very much a part of Israelite society, and play major roles in the narrative. This becomes evident only when we look at the stories of characters with disabilities across the entire Bible, rather than focus on individual verses, or clusters of verses that refer to the disabled.[9] Applying disability studies to the Bible thus allows us to once again read the Bible anew, and opens up possibilities for educational, ethical, and sociological contributions to all of biblical studies.

Those engaging in applying disability studies methodology to the biblical text have focused on the fact that disability is a major theme in the Book of Genesis. Rebeccah Raphael has noted that within Genesis we have two patriarchs who become blind (Isaac and Jacob), one who suffers an injury to his leg to the point where he is forced

---

[9] An early attempt to look at biblical characters as "special" may be found in a keynote address by Dr. Morton Siegel, "How Appropriate Jewish Observances Can Address the Special Child's Needs," given at the First National Conference for Jewish Special Education Professionals in 1979.

to limp (Jacob) and a matriarch with weak eyes.[10] That disabling is a major theme in the book is also emphasized by the fact that already in the Garden of Eden, the punishment of the serpent is a disabling one: He loses his legs.[11] Raphael makes the point that disability in Genesis is what allows the action to move forward, and causes us to see God's power in important ways. "Without disability—infertility overcome, deeply ambiguous blindnesses, or interesting limps—Genesis would be almost entirely episodic."[12] Significantly, though, these impairments do not make the individuals into victims.[13] Jacob wins his struggle with the angel, even after he becomes impaired, and both blind patriarchs manage to bless the sons that God has chosen.

It is generally accepted that the ascendancy of the younger son over the older son in Genesis can be understood as Israel having a self-perception of being the younger son in the world.[14] They considered themselves smaller, and weaker, but the one who carried the blessing and the covenanted relationship with God. This reading takes that approach a step further. Not only is Israel the younger son, but Israel is the disabled younger son. Israel is not only weaker and smaller, but also one who is fighting a personal struggle with physical disabilities. Therefore, Israel is even more in need of God's power, and, is that much more admirable, and that much more grateful for accomplishing what is expected.

Prophetic texts describing Israel's return from exile shed further light on this idea.[15] In the vision of the return, prophets describe the

---

[10] Raphael, pp. 54ff. She includes the barren women in Genesis to her list of disabled individuals in the book. As the question of barrenness is outside the scope of this book, I have not included them in this discussion.

[11] Raphael, 56.

[12] Raphael, 81.

[13] Raphael, 79.

[14] Prouser (1999), 13-15.

[15] Olyan, 78ff.

disabled recovering (e.g., Isaiah 35:4-10), and the disabled included in the return to Jerusalem (e.g. Jeremiah 31:7-9). A most interesting prophetic vision in this context includes "the limping one" in the list of types of people that will be brought back to Jerusalem during the return (e.g. Micah 4:6-7; Zephaniah 3:19). Significantly, the word used for "limping one" is the same word used to describe Jacob's condition in Genesis. The fact that the return to Jerusalem calls attention to one with Jacob's condition lends further support to an understanding of Israel in general as the limping one, the disabled one, the one who needs to work that much harder to accomplish. Once again, though, it is significant that the ones who are disabled accomplish, and are included with everyone else.

While the field of disability studies often concentrates on people with physical disabilities, many of its conclusions and issues also pertain to those with learning disabilities. Most institutions and structures in our society are set up for the able-bodied, causing those with physical limitations to feel a heightened sense of their disabilities. So, too, most schools are set up for "average" learners, causing those with alternative learning styles or learning weaknesses to feel inferior. While progress has been made, the Jewish educational establishment needs to work on developing an educational system that fully embraces and allows for multiple intelligences and divergent ways of learning.

Important questions arise when we read the biblical text through an educational lens. Can the Hebrew Bible, our source of unparalleled understanding and wisdom, also become a source of educational and pedagogic insight? In order to answer this question, we will read the Sinai revelation as an educational endeavor (Exodus 19-20; Deuteronomy 4-6).[16] In this reading, God, the Master Teacher, delivers to

---

[16] I recognize that I am using both versions of the Sinai revelation for this analysis. It is to make a point, not to suggest a conflation of the texts.

the Israelite "class" the most important lesson they will ever learn.

God the teacher takes advantage of many very effective pedagogic techniques. First, God arouses the students' investment in the lesson by building on previous experiential learning: "You have seen what I did to the Egyptians, how I bore you on eagles' wings and brought you to me" (Exodus 19:4). Next, God makes the material even more relevant by explaining its practical applications: "Now then, if you will obey Me faithfully and keep My covenant, you shall be My treasured possession among all the peoples" (Exodus 19:5). In other words, there will be rewards if the Israelites adopt the behaviors God has requested. Also recognizing that students learn as well, if not better, from peer instructors, God involves a member of the "class," Moses, to help the Israelites understand the material. Moses' role becomes very important to the Israelites, as they ask Moses, not God, to speak to them: "'You speak to us,' they entreat Moses, 'and we will obey; but let not God speak to us, lest we die'" (Exodus 20:16).

God uses audio and visual aids, including lightning and thunder (Exodus 19:16), to enhance and emphasize the lesson, and perhaps to illustrate aspects of the Divine (Exodus 19:16). In recognition of the importance of variant modalities, God delivers the teaching in both verbal and written forms to accommodate both auditory and visual learners (Deuteronomy 4:13). Although the written version is to be deposited for the future and not read at that time, the use of multiple modalities still stands. In addition, the group of Israelites receives directions to come forward to the front in order to appreciate the lesson. This shows that God recognizes the importance of preferential seating (Deuteronomy 4:11).

God concludes the lesson with two additional, crucial teaching techniques. First, the Master Teacher provides cues to help the Israelites remember the material. For example, the laws for both *mezuzah* and *tefillin*, which immediately follow the Sinai revelation, involve memory aids[17] to help the people absorb and retain their learning (Deuteronomy 6:8-9). In addition, God includes family education when instructing the "students" to transmit the contents of revelation to their children (Deuteronomy 6:7, 20-25).

It is not typical to look for modern pedagogic techniques in the ancient text of the Bible. I do not mean to suggest that the earliest audiences would have been inclined to understand the text through the lens of pedagogy. However, this need not limit our own reading of the Bible. Today, we claim the right and the obligation to interpret and understand the Bible with the help of all the information and methodologies at our disposal, even those not available in the past. A pedagogic reading lends an unusual perspective to our well-known text. In fact, reading the Sinai revelation as a lesson filled with excellent pedagogy taught by a Master Teacher can have a profound impact on our theological understanding of the event. We can come to see God sensitively adjusting for different kinds of learners, and truly desiring that the message of revelation not only be heard, but understood by all. God does not simply deliver the message to the Israelites, but rather, actively teaches them the material. Understanding God as a Master Teacher can and should have an impact on our view of educators and the reverence they deserve. Further, if God is a Master Teacher, educators may see themselves as working in God's image.

We have seen that applying pedagogic techniques and insights to biblical studies can enhance our understanding of the text. Adding

---

[17] *Mezuzah* refers to a typically decorative container for scriptural passages that Jews are commanded to affix to all doorways of their homes. *Tefillin*, or phylacteries, are black boxes that contain key prayers. During weekday morning prayers, worshipers bind them to their heads and arms via leather straps.

the issue of disability to the discussion leads to additional perspectives and insights. Every reading of text requires some hermeneutic, some approach to interpretation. Often, the hermeneutic is routine and unselfconscious. In this book, the hermeneutic is new and openly applied. It attempts to look at the text by investigating disabilities that may affect certain characters, thereby re-reading the experiences of individuals in the Bible and drawing new theological conclusions about the role of God in their lives. My conclusions about the Bible and its understanding of those with special needs will also add to an understanding of the role of special education in Jewish tradition and in our society.

Esau and ADHD

Esau, the son of Isaac and Rebekah, grandson of Abraham and Sarah, plays a peripheral, subordinate role in Genesis, particularly since his twin brother, Jacob, receives and passes on the patriarchal blessing. As depicted in the Bible, Esau is not a particularly negative character; however, biblical interpreters have developed a fuller, more critical picture of Esau. Rabbinic literature transforms Esau into a man with nefarious motives and an evil character. The Midrash depicts Esau as an idol worshiper from before birth[18] and labels him a *rasha*, or "evil doer" throughout his life.[19] This characterization stems in part from the view of Midrash Rabbah on Genesis, which casts Esau as the embodiment of Rome. The Rabbis of the Talmud believed that the narratives of the ancestors prefigured the historical experiences of their descendants. As part of this thinking, Esau became a symbol for Rome, and to him were attributed all of the evils associated with that empire.[20] Criticism of Esau carries through to modern scholarship as well. "Esau's speech and action mark him as a primitive person. . . Jacob, on the other hand, is as shrewd as Esau is dull-witted."[21]

A careful reading of the biblical text through the lens of special education yields a different picture of Esau. Esau exhibits traits that might lead today to a diagnosis of attention deficit hyperactivity disorder (ADHD).[22] Symptoms of ADHD include hyperactivity, distract-

---

[18] See, e.g., *Bereshit Rabbah* 63; *Yalkut Shimoni* on *Vayetze*.

[19] *Bereshit Rabbah* 63, 65.

[20] Neusner, 28-31.

[21] Berlin, 39.

[22] Shelly Lanzkowsky asserts that her father, a pediatric hematologist, understood Esau as having ADHD, and briefly makes mention of some of the same arguments used in this chapter. Lanzkowsky, 721. Esau also plays a role as a model for a student in a special needs class in an early twentieth century book on educational methods with the

ibility, impulsiveness, and a lack of social consciousness.[23]

The text first introduces us to Esau and his twin, Jacob, even before they are born. Their mother, Rebekah, has a difficult pregnancy, with such excessive fetal movement that she goes to inquire of God, "If this be so, why do I exist?" (Genesis 25:22). This description of a painful pregnancy is unique in the Bible. (Other references to pain in child-birth refer to delivery, not the pregnancy itself.[24]) The fact that many mothers of ADHD children report a similar, uncomfortably high level of fetal activity during their pregnancies supports our hypothesis.[25]

The Hunter and His High Activity Level

The Bible's next reference to Esau is as "a man who knew the hunt, a man of the field" (Genesis 25:27). Esau prefers to be outside and physically active, as opposed to his brother, Jacob, who spends his time sitting in the tent. Esau develops his intense desire to be out-doors into a productive skill and becomes a successful hunter. No-tably, researchers have observed that many of the traits of ADHD are exhibited by people who excel at hunting: A hunter needs to be very focused on his prey, and at the same time, attuned to any movement, however slight, around him. "An individual with the ADD collec-tion of characteristics would make an extraordinarily good hunter. A failure to have any of those characteristics might mean death in the forest or jungle."[26] This innate combination of intense concentration and easy distractibility often occurs in individuals with ADHD, as they

---

title *Blessing Esau*. This title is remarkably close to the title of this book though it only came to my attention serendipitiously very shortly before the manuscript went to print. Randall even goes so far as to call her students "Esaus." Randall, 30ff.

[23] Smith and Strick, 34-40.

[24] See, e.g., Genesis 3:16; Isaiah13:8; Jeremiah 6:14.

[25] Boyles and Contadino, 12; see also Wender, 17.

[26] Hartmann, 17.

may be hyperfocused when they find material interesting, and easily distracted when something more interesting arises.[27] Thus, Esau's hunting prowess supports a view of him as an individual with ADHD. Esau's story becomes all the more poignant when we realize that hunting not only allows him to provide food for his beloved father, but also to achieve success.

Impulsivity and Understanding of Consequences

The next window into Esau's personality opens when he trades his birthright for a pot of stew. Esau comes in from the fields famished and exhausted and asks Jacob for some of the stew he is cooking. Is it possible that he comes home so hungry because he forgot to plan ahead and prepare provisions for his hunting expedition?[28] Jacob offers Esau the food in exchange for his birthright. Jacob's suggestion is shocking, given that the birthright allowed the eldest to inherit significantly more than any siblings. This is a decision that could truly affect his entire future. Esau's birthright is incredibly precious. Despite this, Esau is so overtaken by his hunger that he does not reckon his birthright's true value, and sells it to Jacob. The Bible sums up the encounter with this critique: "Thus did Esau despise the firstborn-right" (Genesis 25:34).

If we consider that Esau has symptoms of ADHD, this scene may be understood somewhat differently. Esau has returned ravenous from his hunting expediton: He needs food and cannot delay gratification. His "impulsive personality is brilliantly portrayed by the use of four rapid-fire verbs."[29] "He *ate* and *drank* and *arose* and *went off*" (Genesis 25:34). Several classic ADHD symptoms are evident: impulsiveness,

---

[27] Wender, 14.
[28] Lanzkosky, 721.
[29] Fox (1995), 117.

craving, and distractibility.[30] One characteristic of ADHD is impulsive decision-making without thought to long-term consequences. "Hunters sometimes totally disregard the long-term consequences of their behavior, so strong is the urge to 'get' whatever they want or 'do it now.'"[31] Does Esau sell his birthright, eat, and then leave because the birthright is not important to him, or does he simply satisfy his craving, get distracted, and move on? Adele Berlin has noted the difference between Esau's actions and the narrator's evaluation of these actions. "To the narrator, Esau disdained the birthright, treated it with contempt. But from Esau's point of view it is not a contemptuous or rebellious action, but one done out of ignorance and shortsightedness."[32] Reading the text through the lens of special needs, we might posit that Esau is neither ignorant nor shortsighted, but simply distractible, a trait that leads to severe consequences for his future.

Appropriate Social Behavior and Social Consciousness

Jacob steals Esau's blessing by dressing up in Esau's clothing and impersonating his brother before their blind father, Isaac (Genesis 27:18). The context of this incident is important. Just prior to this, the text records that Esau has married two Hittite women and that "they were a bitterness of spirit to Isaac and Rebekah" (Genesis 26:34-35). Nowhere in the text has Esau been explicitly instructed *not* to marry Hittite women. On the contrary, it seems that Esau has been expected to absorb this unspoken family principle. When Rebekah seeks to save Jacob from Esau's anger, she tells Isaac that they must send Jacob away to find an appropriate wife from within the family, lest her

---

[30] Significantly, one example of the way hyperactivity manifests in adulthood according to ADHD literature is getting up from the table the second dinner is finished (Wender 19-20).

[31] Hartmann, 42.

[32] Berlin, 39.

favored son *also* marry a Hittite woman, an abhorrence. This may be the first time Esau has heard of this idea. When Esau realizes that his father is unhappy with his marriages to Hittite women, he goes and marries Ishmael's daughter, a relative (Genesis 28:6-9). Poor Esau still can't get it right. Although this marriage is one that Isaac might not have wanted for his son either, from Esau's point of view, marriage to Abraham's granddaughter is an act of true endogamy.[33]

From the foregoing evidence, we can see that Esau does not seem to have a strong sense of proper and appropriate social behavior. He needs to be told directly what others seem able to infer. This is a classic characteristic of ADHD. The text does not portray Esau's motives in marrying the Hittite women as rebelliousness, or as flouting family values. Instead, his marriages can be viewed as the unfortunate products of ignorance. It is also possible to see these marriages as exemplars of Esau's impulsive behavior, a characteristic of ADHD. Impulsiveness may exhibit itself in adulthood through short-lived or multiple relationships and marriages. Along these lines, it may be that Esau has simply married the Hittite women quickly, without much forethought.[34]

Accommodation

Although Esau's family has not given him the extra direction he might have needed in order to make appropriate marriages, Isaac seems to understand Esau's deficiencies and makes an attempt to accommodate his son's special needs. We see this when Isaac gives Esau

---

[33] Although Ishmael is Abraham's legitimate son, Ishmael's daughters are not legitimate marriage partners for descendants of Abraham from the perspective of biblical laws of endogamy. For one thing, Ishmael was expelled from the family. Also, it has been theorized that his birth does not carry divine favor because it occurs before Abraham is circumcised (Kunin 77).

[34] Wender, 21.

instructions to go hunting: "So now, pray pick up your weapons—your hanging-quiver and your bow—go out into the field and hunt me down some hunted-game, and make me a delicacy, such as I love; bring it to me, and I will eat it, that I may give you my own blessing before I die" (Genesis 27:3-4). Isaac's directions are excessive. Why is it necessary to itemize Esau's weapons and tell him to collect them prior to hunting? Wouldn't a skilled hunter know what to do? Would he leave without his weapons? Would he not know which ones he needs? It may be that, in this case, Isaac recognizes that Esau requires explicit directions. Esau must be reminded of that which others would assume.[35] This dynamic is brought into sharper focus when Rebekah recounts Isaac's requirements to Jacob. Her concise version of Isaac's instructions highlights the elaborate quality of Isaac's speech. She quotes her husband as saying, "Bring me some hunted-game and make me a delicacy, I will eat it and give you blessing before YHWH, before my death" (Genesis 27:7). Perhaps Rebekah does not want to accentuate Esau's talent for hunting, a quality Jacob lacks. Isaac's expansive language, however, shows that he has learned how to speak to Esau to help his son understand, respond, and succeed. In this reading, Isaac's insight into Esau's special need illustrates the love and devotion between father and son.

Command/Fulfillment

An element of biblical literary style is "command/fulfillment." When an individual is asked to do something and fulfills the command correctly, the same verb or verbs occur in both the command and fulfillment. However, when different verbs occur in the command and its fulfillment, even when the verbs are synonymous, failure may

---

[35] Boyles and Contadino, 71.

be indicated.[36] One example of the command/fulfillment pattern stands out in Genesis 27:3-5 when the text reports that Isaac asks Esau to "*go out (v'tzeh)* into the field" and Esau "*went off (va-yelekh)* into the field." The use of two different Hebrew roots in Isaac's command to Esau to go hunting, *yatsa* and Esau's fulfillment of it, *halakh*, signals to the reader that Esau will *not* be successful. The mismatch between the language of Isaac's command and Esau's fulfillment of it may also indicate that Esau has difficulty following multiple directions to the letter. By contrast, Jacob precisely fulfills the commands that his mother makes later in the same chapter. The text expresses his actions (*va-yelekh, va-yikach*) with the same language as his mother's orders (*lekh, kach*) (Genesis 27:13-14).

Importance of Parent/Child Bond

It is possible to discern several symptoms of ADHD in the poignant encounter between Esau and Isaac. When Jacob enters the room dressed as Esau, he says only, "My father" (Genesis 27:18). However, when Esau enters Isaac's room for the same purpose, Esau says, "Let my father arise and eat of his son's hunted game so that you yourself may bless me (Genesis 27:31). In this scene, Esau exhibits both an expansive style and an impulsive nature, which leads him to try to attain his goals as quickly as possible.

When he learns that he has been cheated out of the blessing, Esau's reaction is full of pathos and sadness. He cries out bitterly and begs his father for his blessing. He cannot accept that Isaac has only one blessing to give, and repeatedly pleads for another. After the painful encounter, Esau, filled with anger and thoughts of revenge, plans to

---

[36] For an excellent discussion of types of repetition in biblical narrative, see Sternberg, 365-440.

kill Jacob—but only after the death of their father.

Given Esau's impulsiveness, he shows an impressive ability to control himself after learning that he has been duped. He is angry enough to murder his brother, but devoted enough to his father to delay his plan (Genesis 27:41). Esau's ability to restrain himself from killing Jacob immediately, despite his ADHD, is worthy of note and highlights the depth of his feelings for his father.[37]

Leaving the Past in the Past

Esau's strong anger dissipates, although the text is silent about the time frame for its resolution. By the time of Esau's reunion with Jacob many years later, Esau expresses only love and joy (Genesis 33:4-16). Jacob, however, is the one who is more affected by their shared history. He initiates an exchange of gifts with Esau, first sending messengers to notify Esau that he is on his way, and that he has become very successful monetarily (Genesis 32:4-6). It appears that his initial instinct and knowledge of Esau's behavior leads him to believe that Esau would have calmed down by now and be open to a reunion.[38] Upon hearing that Esau is traveling with four hundred men, however, Jacob becomes very afraid that Esau is still in the grips of a murderous rage. Jacob's concern is not unfounded. His last family memory was one of fleeing for his life (Genesis 27:43). In addition, the experience of human nature he has acquired has taught him that people do not simply forget the past. He sees his wives living daily with considerable

---

[37] The motivation for Esau's impulse control is his intense love for his father. We should not assume from this that Esau would now be able to control himself in every situation. Often, a false expectation is generated when a person with ADHD successfully restrains his behavior. It is a mistake to assume that since the person had success in one situation, he or she should be able to show similar control in all circumstances. The preferable response is to exhibit admiration and respect for the individual regarding his or her handling of the one event rather than raise expectations which can not be met.

[38] Spero, 248.

and lasting tension that stems, at least in part, from the marriage ruse that Laban manufactured (Genesis 29:20-29). Jacob also engages in a number of struggles with Laban, which, despite a quick treaty, never truly resolve (Genesis 31).

We further witness Jacob's own inability to "forgive and forget" when he "blesses" his children upon his deathbed. There, he holds them accountable for all of their previous misdeeds (Genesis 49). In sum, life has taught Jacob that people hold grudges. Perhaps it is Jacob's own guilty feelings about how he treated his brother and father that add to his apprehension about seeing Esau again. His persistent guilt may foster the expectation that Jacob should still be punished for his actions.

Esau's friendly greeting turns out to be the opposite of what Jacob expects. Esau's ADHD-like symptoms may help explain this warm response. Individuals with ADHD often experience very strong and extreme moods of short duration. This is especially true of feelings of anger. "ADHD anger is generally very different from the brooding, continuous anger seen in borderline patients, and from the chronic anger and irritability seen in some patients with major depression. In ADHD patients, the anger often seems provoked from a stimulus rather than released from a persisting source."[39] Further, though the anger may be very strong, it tends to dissipate surprisingly quickly. This analysis fits very well with Esau's previous conduct, and with the reunion scene: Esau meets his brother again with the apparent desire to renew a fraternal bond. (More about Jacob's response due to his *own* disability in a later chapter.)

---

[39] Wender, 29.

Social Blindness

A further point about ADHD arises from the way Esau understands Jacob's offerings and responses during the reunion. Jacob approaches Esau with fear, hesitation, caution, and wariness (Genesis 33:1-3). Esau, on the other hand, runs over to his brother, and hugs and kisses him through tears. His invitation to Jacob to join his group, under the assumption that a long-term reunion is what both of them desire, shows Esau's serious lack of interpersonal insight. One major characteristic of ADHD is a social cognitive deficit. This deficit finds expression in many different behaviors. For example, individuals with ADHD may not understand social cues, or may have difficulty with social prediction. They may not be able to interpret the nuances of facial expressions. They may have "social blindness," which can lead them to rush into situations better approached with caution and forethought. They may misinterpret feedback from others. Poor social memory, including the inability to recall prior social experiences or to learn from them may also exist.[40]

Social deficit is evident in this late encounter between Jacob and Esau. Esau does not seem to understand Jacob's hesitation, or the purpose of his gifts: Esau asks, "What to you is all this camp that I have met?" (Genesis 33:8). Esau does not realize that Jacob has no desire to live with him. Esau heads into the meeting expecting a beautiful, long-awaited family reunion. He finds past problems irrelevant for understanding their present relationship. While Esau's expectations appear noble, Esau is naive to expect that Jacob will feel completely comfortable, especially since the last thing Jacob heard about his brother was that Esau planned to kill him (Genesis 27:41-42). Had Esau given more thought to overcoming his troubled history with his

---

[40] Selikowitz, 48-54.

brother, he might have begun by assuring Jacob of his peaceful inten-
tions, or trying to ease the tension. However, he does no such thing.

We find an instructive parallel scene in Joseph's reunion with his
brothers in Egypt. Joseph does not ignore the past. Far from it. Joseph
understands the need to reassure his brothers that he does not hold
a grudge for their terrible behavior toward him. He recognizes his
brothers' concerns and discomfort, and repeatedly emphasizes that
he does not continue to hold them responsible for their heartlessness
toward him, but rather ascribes events to God's plan (Genesis 45:3-8).
In our current reunion story, on the other hand, Esau acts as if past
events did not occur, or at least, have no bearing on the present. The
tense reunion scene thus supports a view of Esau as having ADHD.

Addressing the Issue

How does it affect our reading to view Esau as having symptoms of
ADHD? Clearly, we are able to explain Esau's impulsive behavior, the
ease with which he is distracted, and his desire to be active in the out-
of-doors. We can imagine that the very characteristics for which he is
reviled in later literature may be the result of a neurological condition.
Consider the life Esau could have led had he been understood and
nurtured with appropriate care. How different would the story have
been if Esau had been trained properly as to whom it was appropriate
to marry and as to what was most important to his family. In Esau's
case, we should view the Bible not as a model for proper approaches
to ADHD, but as a cautionary tale about the improper approach. It is a
reading to sensitize us, so that today's "Esaus" may be spared "a very
great and bitter cry" (Genesis 27:34).

Isaac and mental retardation

Isaac is a difficult character to get to know. Overshadowed by his father Abraham, his son Jacob, and his wife Rebekah, many scholars see him as a virtual "non-character."

> "Yitzhak functions in Genesis as a classic second generation—that is, as a transmitter and stabilizing force, rather than as an active participant in the process of building the people. There hardly exists a story about him in which he is anything but a son and heir, a husband, or a father. What this means, unfortunately, is that he has almost no personality of his own."[41]

Others have referred to Isaac as "more or less the plaything of others' interests."[42]

There are more flattering readings of Isaac, which note that he is more than a mere transition between Abraham and Jacob. The biblical account does contain unmistakable elements of individuality. Isaac's name, uniquely bestowed by God, is not changed; his pastoral wanderings are restricted to a narrow range; he alone remains monogamous; he is the only patriarch to engage in agriculture and the only one never to leave the promised land; finally, the unique divine name *pachad yitzchak* (Genesis 31:42) suggests some episode, not recorded, in which this particular name would have been meaningful.[43]

Despite the enigmatic picture of Isaac in the Bible, he clearly is unique. As he is one of the three patriarchs in the Book of Genesis, he is in elite company. Within Jewish tradition, he is respected for his fi-

---

[41] Fox (1995), 111.
[42] Martin-Achard, 464.
[43] Sarna, 177.

delity to God and to the covenant, for his devotion to the land, and for the love he shows to his family. At the same time, his character pales in contrast to other figures in the Genesis narratives. Is he a weak character with little to contribute, or is his story simply absent from the Bible for some other reason? Abundant textual evidence suggests that Isaac may be analyzed as an individual with symptoms of mild mental retardation. Reading Isaac's story in this way throws new light on his frustratingly vague characterization. It transforms our sense of his capabilities, his life, and gives us a new understanding of what God expects of him.[44]

What Kind of Laughter...?

Support for the theory that Isaac is mentally challenged appears right from the beginning of Isaac's life. He is born to older parents, who are close relatives, a genetic heritage that can result in birth defects. At Isaac's birth, Sarah makes a peculiar statement: "God has made laughter for me; all who hear of it will laugh for me" (Genesis 21:6). This verse is complex because the Hebrew is ambiguous. Would all who hear of Isaac's birth laugh for joy at the new life Sarah has created, or laugh at her in ridicule? Has God given her reason to rejoice, or reason to feel mocked and humiliated?[45] Perhaps Sarah has to cope with the mixed feelings that can plague a parent who has a child with a disability? She has waited until the age of 90 to become pregnant, and the result of this "miraculous" birth is a disabled child. In this reading, it is not surprising to find in Sarah's first response to the baby

---

[44] The same conclusion was drawn in Judith Z. Abrams, "Was Isaac Disabled," 20-21. Kaminsky also draws this conclusion, but understands Isaac as a "bumbler and dullard," leading the text to be understood in comedic terms.

[45] Robert Alter notes that there is a hint here that God has made Sarah into a laughingstock (Alter, *Genesis*, 97). Some traditional rabbinic commentaries seem to go out of their way to protect Sarah, perhaps in response to the same ambiguity in the text.

feelings of shock and humiliation.[46]

Sarah soon moves beyond her initial reaction and becomes a fiercely devoted and protective mother. It is typical of parents of the mentally retarded, particularly mothers, to overprotect their children. Often, these parents intuitively sense their children's special requirements and difficulties, and lovingly try to make their lives as easy as possible.[47] Sarah's overprotective tendencies become especially prominent in her behavior toward her servant, Hagar, and Hagar's son Ishmael. During the years of Sarah's barrenness prior to Isaac's birth, Sarah gave Hagar to Abraham as a wife in order to become a mother of children through her (Genesis 16:1-6).[48] Since Hagar is Sarah's servant, according to the customs set forth in Genesis, Sarah has the power to give Hagar to Abraham as a second wife. Any children Hagar produces with Abraham are officially considered offspring of Sarah. Hagar's son Ishmael is therefore Abraham's son, and a possible heir. When Sarah sees Ishmael "laughing," she insists that Hagar and Ishmael be sent away so that Ishmael will not inherit Abraham's property together with Isaac (Genesis 21:9-10).

The text does not explain why Ishmael's behavior offends Sarah. One reading suggests that Ishmael is mocking Isaac in some way. It also has been suggested that Ishmael is playing innocently.[49] *Metsachek*, the Hebrew word that describes Ishmael's behavior, can reflect different meanings, ranging from joyous laughter to sexual behavior.

---

[46] This reading raises the question of whether Sarah could have known of the disability right from Isaac's birth. While in many cases parents are not aware of the mental retardation until some time after birth, many parents speak of having a "feeling" that something is wrong right from the beginning.

[47] Flanigan, Baker, and LaFollette, 81.

[48] For other examples of this practice in Genesis, see Rachel and Leah's conduct in Genesis 30:3, 9.

[49] Fox translates the verb as *laughing*, but notes that it is perhaps *mockingly* (Fox (1995) 89). Alter notes that interpretations of this verb have ranged from references to homosexual activity to mocking laughter (Alter, *Genesis* 98).

Although many readers assume that Ishmael has aroused Sarah's anger by doing something that involves Isaac, it is important to note that the verse does not contain an object for the verb *metsachek*. In other words, it seems more likely that Ishmael is doing something by himself. We can also read *metsachek* as "acting like Isaac (Y*itzchack*)," in the sense that Ishmael is trying to *be* Isaac, with all that means in terms of inheritance.[50] In this reading, Isaac is neither party to, nor the object of, Ishmael's activity.

Given Sarah's feelings about Hagar and her offspring, it is certainly possible that Ishmael has done absolutely nothing wrong. It may be that Sarah sees Ishamel's very existence as a threat to Isaac and that is enough for her to insist that Ishmael and his mother be sent away.[51] Although Sarah's banishment of Hagar and Ishmael is difficult to accept, reading Sarah as the overprotective mother of a mentally retarded child allows us to alter our perception and perhaps even sympathize with her. It may be that the best way Sarah can think of to care for Isaac is to remove all of the obstacles in his way. A mentally retarded man described this dynamic in very poignant terms:

> Sometimes I think the pain of being handicapped
> is that people give you so much love that it becomes a
> weight on you and a weight on them. There is no way
> that you can break from it without hurting them—
> without bad feelings—guilt.[52]

As we will see, Sarah's ferocious maternal attempts to shield Isaac from pain and trouble unfortunately lead him to develop a great dependence on his parents that lasts throughout his life.[53]

---

[50] Alter *Genesis,* 98.
[51] Ibid.
[52] Bogdan and Taylor, 37.
[53] Flanigan, Baker, and LaFollette, 81.

ISAAC AND MENTAL RETARDATION

Isaac Bound

After Isaac's birth, the Bible moves into one of its most famous episodes, the binding of Isaac (Genesis 22). Rabbis, scholars, and students have tried to understand how Isaac could have so willingly and innocently gone along with Abraham on the journey. Can't Isaac see what is happening? If we understand Isaac as a mildly retarded individual who is unusually dependent on his parents, the story becomes more plausible. In the harrowing narrative, Isaac is passive and trusting. His docility is evident even in the language of the text: Isaac is the object of verbs; his father Abraham places the things he needs to carry directly onto him (Genesis 22:6). Isaac does not even take the initiative to pick up the wood they will use to build a fire for the sacrifice. He questions his father in only the simplest terms, and seems to draw comfort from Abraham's superficial and evasive answer (Genesis 22: 7-8). This is not to say that Isaac is wholly unaware of what is happening around him. However, his complete faith and trust in his parents precludes him from probing more extensively.[54]

Marriage and Beyond

Isaac's passivity and dependence continue in his marriage. Notably, Abraham arranges for his servant to leave and find a wife for Isaac.[55]

---

[54] Kaminsky notes that it takes three days for Isaac to ask his question, which supports the theory of Isaac's mental deficiency. He also finds humor in Abraham toying with Isaac by claiming that God will provide the lamb. He sees this as an example of the type of comedy that includes a wiser, craftier person taking advantage of one who is of lesser intelligence (368). I don't see this as working with the larger picture of the Akedah. This text will be discussed further in Chapter 4.

[55] Kaminsky notes that perhaps there was a concern that no one would want to marry Isaac, and therefore, Abraham sent his servant alone. In addition, he claims that the test given to discover the identity of the bride, that is, that she would offer water to him and his camels, was simple, and not demanding. In other words, the idea is that anyone would pass that test, and they were specifically not being choosy as they were concerned about Isaac's ability to marry (369).

Isaac is the only patriarch whose marriage plans take place in the text, but who does not take part in those arrangements.[56] Abraham's servant locates Rebekah, an appropriate wife from the extended family, and brings her back to Isaac. Her first meeting with Isaac is significant for the present reading. "He lifted up his eyes and saw: here, camels coming! Rebekah lifted up her eyes and saw Isaac... brought her into the tent of Sara his mother, he took Rebekah and she became his wife, and he loved her. Thus was Isaac comforted after his mother" (Genesis 24:63-64, 67). These verses are striking, showing that Rebekah and Isaac do not see the same thing in the same way. Whereas Isaac looks up and sees camels, Rebekah looks up and sees Isaac. Isaac sees simply what is squarely in front of him, while Rebekah discerns the larger picture and its significance.[57]

One characteristic of mildly retarded individuals is difficulty organizing a variety of stimuli into a meaningful whole.[58] Along these lines, Isaac does not yet comprehend that the caravan he sees in the distance relates to him and will change his life. However, this fact does not stop him from loving Rebekah upon meeting her. Subsequently, Isaac brings Rebekah into his mother's tent and finally feels relief from the pain of his mother's death. The text very quickly casts Rebekah in Sarah's role. With Isaac's mother and protector gone, Rebekah takes over as Isaac's support and guide. Many individuals with mental retardation tend to seek out a non-retarded "benefactor" for

---

[56] Although we know little about Abraham's own marital beginnings, it is not stated that his father has arranged the match.

[57] Raphael understands this asymmetry in Isaac's and Rebekah's visual abilities as the beginning of Isaac's blindness. She sees him as the first person not to be affected by Rebekah's beauty, and thus, as one who needs to use other senses and not his vision in order to make his way in the world (67-68). She also notes that all around Isaac, people are described as hearing, thus emphasizing a sense that was probably more used by Isaac (72).

[58] Flanigan, Baker, and LaFollette, 94.

advice and help.[59] Rebekah plays this role for Isaac, filling the gap left by his mother's death.

Isaac and the Land

Another significant detail in Isaac's betrothal narrative is Abraham's concern that Isaac not leave the land. The servant whom Abraham sends to find a wife for his son expresses concern that a woman might not follow him home without seeing her suitor, in which case he would have to bring Isaac to the woman's family. But Abraham adamantly insists that Isaac remain in Canaan (Genesis 24:5-6). God repeats this sentiment later, when Isaac and Rebekah wish to move to Egypt because of famine. Since Abraham traveled to Egypt at the time of an earlier famine, Isaac has in mind a similar plan. However, God assures Isaac of divine protection and explicitly demands that Isaac should remain in Canaan rather than go down to Egypt (Genesis 26:2-3). Why is it so important that Isaac stay in the land? Both Abraham and God do not want Isaac to quit his familiar surroundings. Perhaps they worry that he may not readily adapt to a new situation or function well in a new environment.

When a famine occurs, God allows Isaac to travel as far as Gerar (Genesis 26:1-5). While there, to protect himself and his wife, Isaac attempts the same deception as his father (Genesis 12:10-20; 20:1-18), claiming that his wife is his sister: "But it was, when he had been there a long time, that Avimelekh, king of the Philistines, looked out through a window and saw: there was Isaac laughing-and-loving with Rivka his wife!" (Genesis 26:8).[60] Earlier in the text, when Abra-

---

[59] Baroff, 41.

[60] This scene repeats itself three times in the Book of Genesis, twice with Abraham and Sarah (Genesis 12, 20), and once with Isaac and Rebekah. While some scholarly methodological approaches focus on the repetition of the narrative, it is of equal interest to make note of the differences that crop up in each of the tellings.

ham perpetrates this ruse against the king of Egypt, the king does not discover that Abraham and Sarah are married until God tells him. Unlike his father, Isaac is not successful at duping the Philistine king. Isaac acts intimately with his wife in public at the very time that he is trying to conceal the fact of his marriage! Isaac does not seem to understand that this behavior will likely give away his true marital status. It is also clear from the text that it is Isaac's actions, not Rebekah's, that lead to their being caught. Further, when the king confronts Isaac, Isaac does not try to talk his way out of trouble, like Abraham did (Genesis 20:11-13). Isaac either is too afraid to respond properly, or is not mentally quick enough to find the right words. Isaac's notably short, simplistic answer to the king expresses only his fear that he will be killed.

Isaac exhibits poor social acuity and communication skills in his further dealings with the Philistines. When Isaac becomes very wealthy and Abimelech, king of Gerar, asks him to leave, Isaac obeys immediately (Genesis 26:16-17). Then Isaac enters into a conflict with Philistine shepherds over the ownership of various wells. However, he continues to back away from every confrontation, and when the shepherds complain, he leaves and digs a new well. In short, he does not seem comfortable engaging in disputes. Fortunately, Isaac is aware of his passive nature and continues to search until he finds a place where he can live without conflict (Genesis 26:22).

Blessing

A view of Isaac as a person with symptoms of mental retardation provides a new window into God's relationship with the second Patriarch. God accepts Isaac as a man who is very different from Abraham and allows him to find success in areas that are not beyond his reach.

In God's revelation to Isaac, God repeats the blessing of Abraham. Isaac will be blessed and will have innumerable offspring, by whom all others will be blessed (Genesis 26:2-5). However, God gives the blessing on Abraham's merit, saying, "I will fulfill the sworn-oath that I swore to Avraham your father: I will make your seed many, like the stars of the heavens, and to your seed I will give all these lands; all the nations of the earth shall enjoy blessing through your seed—in consequence of Avraham's hearkening to my voice and keeping my charge: my commandments, my laws, and my instructions" (Genesis 26:3-5). Notably, Isaac's blessing differs from the blessing his father received in that it does not give conditions that Isaac must fulfill. Rather, the blessing takes any onus off Isaac because it derives from Abraham's worthy deeds.

Nevertheless, Isaac fulfills God's order not to leave the land, the single command he receives directly from God. As a result, God helps Isaac become very successful in agriculture (Genesis 26:12),[61] allowing Isaac to shine within his limited scope. God's relationship with Isaac is very one-sided. Isaac does not initiate any part of the relationship with the Deity, and is far more passive around God than are Abraham and Jacob. In addition, in the Isaac narrative, God is called *pachad yitschak*, "The Terror of Isaac" (Genesis 31:42).[62] This is a difficult term whose meaning may include a combination of fear and awe.[63] Given Isaac's near-sacrifice to this God, it is reasonable to expect that he would feel great fear in his dealings with the Divine.

---

[61] It has been shown that in less technologically advanced societies, intellectual limitations are less of a drawback since there are more areas of life in which a person can succeed (Baroff, 13).

[62] The use of this term is all the more striking as in the same verse, God is referred to as *elohei Avraham*, "The God of Abraham."

[63] This difficult phrase has been interpreted several different ways, including as "the fear of Isaac," and "the thigh of Isaac." According to the second interpretation it would be related to the patriarchal oaths that were accompanied by a touching of the thigh of another. For a fuller discussion, see Meir Malul, "More on Pahad Yishaq."

It is also possible, however, that the term indicates Isaac's inability to comprehend his relationship with God, beyond feelings of fear and awe. Unlike his father, Isaac never achieves a mature relationship with God, one that involves give and take, discussion, questioning, and understanding. Instead, he simply attempts to follow God's directions to the best of his ability.

The Family Unit

Isaac's relationship with Rebekah and their children further supports the idea that he can be seen as mildly developmentally disabled. From the moment they are married, Rebekah dominates the family. She is very active and assertive and does not seem to involve Isaac in the family's affairs. For instance, when she has a difficult pregnancy, she consults an oracle, not her husband, to find out what is wrong (Genesis 25:22-24). It is very significant that she never shares the oracle's words with Isaac. After they have twins, Isaac and Rebekah each favor a different child. "Isaac grew to love Esau, for (he brought) hunted-game for his mouth, but Rebekah loved Jacob" (Genesis 25:28). Scholars have suggested that the juxtaposition of these phrases shows Rebekah's unconditional, parental love for Jacob, as opposed to Isaac's love for Esau, which is a response to a specific behavior (hunting). Given the beautiful, devoted relationship between Esau and Isaac that appears in the next chapter of the Bible, this description of Isaac's love for his son seems shallow or lacking. Perhaps Isaac cannot adequately describe his feelings for Esau, and it is this deficiency, rather than the absence of deep love, that the narrator highlights.

Isaac's preference for Esau makes even greater sense if we also think of Isaac as disabled. Studies of families in which a parent has a developmental disability have found that in some cases, the parents are more comfortable with their less intelligent children.[64] The higher the child's intelligence, the greater the alienation of the mentally disabled parent. Given what we know of both sons, it is likely that Isaac would have felt greater ease with Esau than with Jacob. After all, Esau was duped twice, once into selling the birthright and once having his blessing stolen, and seems to have some difficulty keeping up with his brighter brother.

This reading of Isaac also sheds new light on the famous episode in which Jacob, with Rebekah's help, steals the blessing from Esau. Although Rebekah has known of Jacob's destiny to supersede his brother even before their birth, she has not shared the information with Isaac. When Isaac calls for Esau to prepare a meal so that he may give him the family blessing, Rebekah can wait no longer to act. She prepares food, dresses Jacob in Esau's garments and sends him in to his father masquerading as Esau: "He came to his father and said: Father! He said: Here I am. Which one are you, my son? Jacob said to his father: I am Esau, your firstborn. I have done as you spoke to me: Pray arise, sit and eat from my hunted-game, that you may give me your own blessing" (Genesis 27:18-19). Isaac seems to be fooled by this charade. Despite all the uncertainty, the questions, and the suspicion, Isaac gives Jacob the blessing meant for Esau. There are so many difficulties in this story of deception that scholars have long sought explanations for Isaac's conduct. For example, some have speculated that Isaac knows he should bless Jacob, but cannot bring himself to hurt Esau, whom he loves so deeply. Therefore, Isaac allows himself to be deceived by his wife and son.[65]

Several details from this section of the narrative, and perhaps the

---

[64] Whitman and Accardo, 123-37.
[65] This theory has appeared in various places. See, for example, Prouser, 22-23, and Plaut, 30-34.

entire Isaac cycle, take on remarkable clarity and meaning if we understand Isaac as mildly mentally disabled. Note that he is deceived not once, but twice. Initially, he is tricked into blessing Jacob instead of Esau (Genesis 27:1-29). Thereafter, when Esau threatens to kill Jacob, Rebekah again fools Isaac into sending Jacob away to be married in order to get Jacob safely out of the house (Genesis 27:41-28:5). In addition, Isaac uses a tactile, unsophisticated method of determining which son is standing before him. After Isaac discovers the ruse, his reaction to Esau seems very unsympathetic. Instead of trying to support and comfort his distraught son, Isaac appears genuinely confused and repeatedly emphasizes the irrevocable aspect of the blessing, rubbing salt in Esau's wounds. Only Esau's continued pleas lead Isaac to find him an alternate blessing. Rebekah's position in this story also fits the dominant role she assumes and maintains from the moment she meets Isaac. Since she knows Jacob is the son meant to receive the blessing, and since she must have recognized that Isaac might not see to this destiny, she steps in to make sure that events follow the divine plan. Thus Rebekah's actions need not seem evil or manipulative. Rather, they continue the mission of protection and guidance she has given her mentally challenged husband and their family for so long.

In looking at Isaac from the perspective of developmental disability, he appears not as a "non-character" or as the "plaything of others' interests." Rather, he is a man of integrity and courage. He faces disabilities and deficiencies, yet lives a full life surrounded by a family who loves him. He obeys God's command to remain in his homeland and he passes on the patriarchal blessing to the next generation. Perhaps he does not break new theological ground, and perhaps he contributes to some problematic family dynamics. Despite it all, God's generous blessings lead him to great success at agriculture, and his wife's determined actions help him to continue the patriarchal line. Although Isaac often needs assistance, he carries on with dignity and strength. For these reasons, he deserves our respect. We must strive to emulate God in accepting people's limitations and helping every person to feel the joy of success, regardless of his or her mental or physical capacity.

Family dynamics in families with a disabled member

The Book of Genesis contains many stories of families which depict charged and tense dynamics. Sibling rivalry is ever-present and favoritism and parenting missteps are numerous. Reading emotional, mental, or physical disabilities into these stories can help explain a great deal of this rampant familial strife.

The disability of a family member typically has a strong effect on every individual in the family and on their relationships with one another. This is evident in the families of both Abraham and Isaac. The theory that Isaac has symptoms of mental retardation may help explain how Sarah and Abraham parent. Sarah is a strong character with a large degree of control over her family. While overprotecting Isaac, Sarah conducts herself with a combination of disdain, jealousy, discomfort, and harshness toward Hagar and Ishmael. Certainly, it is fair to challenge Sarah's treatment of Abraham's other son and his mother. However, it is important to keep in mind that God supports and condones Sarah's cruelty (Genesis 16:9, 21:12). It may be that God takes Sarah's side against Hagar and Ishmael because Isaac is mentally retarded.

Protectiveness

In Chapter 2 we posited that Sarah may be naturally overprotective of Isaac due to his developmental delay. Isaac's retardation may also be at the root of the strained relationship between Sarah and Ishmael. Studies have shown that parents not only are overprotective of the child with the disability, but also make excessive demands on the non-handicapped siblings.[66] This would have been especially true of Sarah with regard to Ishmael, as he is so much older than Isaac. Research has also shown that parents have less tolerance for children who mistreat siblings with mental retardation as opposed to those who mistreat siblings possessed of normal cognitive development.[67] This fact can illuminate Sarah's extreme reaction to Ishmael's alleged mocking of Isaac (Genesis 21:9). It may also be that God's apparent acceptance and support of Sarah's behavior shows that God shares Sarah's inclination to protect Isaac. While Sarah's conduct, and God's, remain open to criticism, this new reading may soften our view of the harsh treatment Ishmael receives.

Personality Change in Response
to Having a Child with Disabilities

Parents typically have a variety of reactions to the birth of a disabled child. These can include fear, anger, loneliness, guilt, self-doubt, marital stress, resentment, rejection of the child, and depression, along with acceptance and love.[68] Abraham's behavior before and after the birth of Isaac fits this multi-faceted model. Prior to Isaac's birth, Abraham is notably obedient to God, courageous, kind, and attuned to justice. He follows an unknown God's directions (Genesis 12:1-9), fights for his family's honor and his nephew's life (Genesis 14), extends warm hospitality to strangers (Genesis 18:1-16), and argues with God over the imperative of justice (Genesis 18:17-33). Despite the fact that there are two morally questionable scenes in which he claims that his wife is his sister (Genesis 12,20), the overall picture of

---

[66] Meyer and Vadasy, 25-26.
[67] Ibid.
[68] Alper, Schloss, and Schloss, 59-60.

Abraham is positive, indeed.

Abraham seems to undergo a marked change after the birth of Isaac. He banishes his son, Ishmael, and concubine, Hagar, under God's and Sarah's orders (Genesis 21:10-21); follows without question or argument God's direction to sacrifice Isaac (Genesis 22); and separates himself from Sarah (Genesis 22:19-23:2). At this point in the narrative, Abraham, rather than a self-assured Patriarch, is a lonely man plagued by doubts about his relationship with God. Commentators often struggle with the question of why Abraham argues with God for the lives of the people of Sodom, who are strangers to him, but not on behalf of his own son. Re-reading Abraham as the parent of a disabled child can help make sense of this shift in his behavior.

Abraham and Sarah tread a lengthy path to childbearing that ends with the arrival of Isaac when they are advanced in age. Each experiences the process differently. Sarah feels that she has given Hagar to Abraham as a surrogate, hoping that the child will be hers. However, this plan fails; Ishmael clearly belongs to Hagar, not Sarah. Sarah waits many more years before she is given the opportunity to bear her own child. Abraham's effort to secure an heir is different. Until God informs Abraham that he will have a son of his own (Genesis 15:2-4), Abraham first believes that Lot, and then his servant Eliezer, will succeed him. Abraham's dream comes true when Ishmael, his long-awaited biological child, is born. Abraham loves him and raises him as the covenantal heir. So great is Abraham's love for Ishmael that, upon being told that he will have a son with Sarah, Abraham simply pleads to God, "If only Yishmael might live in your presence!" (Genesis 17:18). Thus, Abraham has invested his hopes and dreams in three "heirs" before Isaac comes along. All of this must heighten and intensify Abraham's expectations and anticipation of Isaac's birth.

The birth of a handicapped child can precipitate a theological crisis for the parents.[69] How much more so when their faith is under development and the child is a long-awaited miracle baby. Following Isaac's birth, Abraham seems to lose confidence in himself and in God's goodness. He withdraws and becomes capable of abandoning the people closest to him, including both wives and both sons, at one time or another. In Sodom prior to Isaac's birth, Abraham confidently argues with God that the conduct of a just and righteous God must be ethical: "Heaven forbid for you to do a thing like this, to deal death to the innocent along with the guilty, that it should come about: like the innocent, like the guilty, Heaven forbid for you! The Judge of all the earth—will He not do what is just?" (Genesis 18:25). However, Abraham's opinion of God changes after Isaac arrives. How can a just God allow loyal and obedient followers to have a disabled child, and how can God allow that innocent child to struggle? How can God make promises that future generations will come through Isaac, if Isaac has deficits? After all the painful waiting, how can God have perpetrated this cruelty upon Abraham and Isaac both? Perhaps it is this crisis of faith that keeps Abraham from developing a loving bond with Isaac. Certainly, there are no signs of closeness or connection between them. Abraham's doubts also may lead to his silence about the Binding of Isaac (referred to as the *Akedah* in Hebrew). Once Abraham begins to believe that he no longer understands God's fundamental qualities, he may no longer have any frame of reference for arguing with God or for interceding on his son's behalf.[70]

---

[69] Powell and Ogle, 34-35.

[70] One must, of course, recognize that there are many different and varied readings of Abraham's role in the *Akedah*. Abraham has been seen as God's obedient servant, as a man who tests God while God tests him, and even as one who fails God's test because he fails to stand up for his son and his family. (See Trible, "Genesis 22: The Sacrifice of Sarah"; Spiegel, *The Last Trial*; Gros Louis "Abraham: II").

Parental Acceptance

After preventing Abraham from sacrificing his son, God repeats the promise that Abraham will have many blessed descendants. For the first time Abraham seems to realize that the blessing is still in effect, even with a disabled child. It is at this point that he arrives at the stage of acceptance for his new son's place in the divine plan. Soon afterwards, Abraham follows up his new insight into Isaac's hopeful future by arranging for Isaac's marriage. This is a sure sign of Abraham's investment in Isaac and renewed confidence in God's master plan (Genesis 24).

What is it about the *Akedah* that makes Abraham suddenly come to terms with and accept his son? A nontraditional understanding of the "test" of the *Akedah* may help explain Abraham's growth. God places Abraham in an unsettling and unclear situation, yet directs him with a voice that Abraham feels compelled to follow and trust. In other words, God has given Abraham a taste of what it means to be Isaac. Isaac often does not understand context and might be fuzzy about long-term goals, but he obeys his father and performs as directed. At Moriah, Abraham enters Isaac's world. Abraham does not know what God wants, and nothing really makes sense. Yet, Abraham uncomprehendingly follows God's command. Perhaps God knows that Abraham can only begin to appreciate his son by experiencing what it might be like to *be* Isaac, however briefly.[71]

Through this traumatic learning experience, Abraham comes to value Isaac and grasp how Isaac fits into God's scheme. Abraham's gradual return to a more comfortable and positive emotional state following the *Akedah* and the death of Sarah is illustrated by his remar-

---

[71] I thank Sheila Silverman for this insight. Special educators have used this same method to show how it feels to be a learning disabled student. See, e.g., the success and widespread use of the movie *F.A.T. City.*

riage and the birth of six more children (Genesis 25:1-7). However, the subsequent children never replace Isaac in Abraham's esteem. Abraham follows in Sarah's footsteps by continuing to protect Isaac and his destiny. Before he dies, Abraham gives each of his new sons gifts and sends them off. However, he saves his full inheritance for Isaac (Genesis 25:6). Perhaps, aware of Isaac's passive nature, Abraham ensures that Isaac will not have to fight any inheritance battles with his half-brothers. Significantly, Abraham neither abandons any of his sons, nor sends them out into the desert as he did with Ishmael. Abraham has matured since he banished Hagar and their child. This time, his children are dispatched with enough in their pockets to live independently. Small wonder that the text says Abraham dies content (Genesis 25:8).

The Strained Marriage

The next generation finds Isaac's family also suffering from significant discord. Isaac and Rebekah share a beautiful love story before their children come along. At the inauguration of their relationship, Isaac loves Rebekah and finds comfort in her presence (Genesis 24:67). Isaac and Rebekah do not interact in the text until many years later, when Isaac prays for a child on Rebekah's behalf. Precisely because of this prayer, God allows Rebekah to become pregnant (Genesis 25:21). Nowhere else in the Bible does a husband pray to end his wife's barrenness, let alone take up her reproductive problems without being asked. Abraham avoids the topic, and Jacob rebukes Rachel when she asks him for help with her infertility (Genesis 30:1-2). Elkanah, Hannah's husband, claims that his love is better than the love of sons ever could be (1 Samuel 1:8).[72]

---

[72] It should be noted that Elkanah's statement to Hannah is quite ambiguous and

Unlike other husbands in the Bible, Isaac senses his wife's distress and tries to help her. His action does not contradict the hypothesis that he may have symptoms of mild retardation. Since the Bible does not spell out the words of his prayer about Rebekah, it might have been a very simple prayer. Whereas other biblical characters deemed it inappropriate to ask God for a gift as great as a child, it may be that Isaac's naiveté allows him to find such a request acceptable. Hannah's example provides a telling contrast. While she also beseeches God for a child, she apologetically includes in her prayer a vow to give the boy to God (1 Samuel 1:11).

Withholding Information

Given the tender beginning of Isaac and Rebekah's relationship, the state of their marriage is startlingly poor by the time Rebekah helps Jacob steal Esau's blessing from Isaac (see Genesis 27). Perhaps Rebekah acts to accomplish what Isaac knows must be done, but cannot do alone. Just as Isaac senses his wife's needs and prays for her to produce children, Rebekah senses her husband's needs and accomplishes the transfer of the blessing to Jacob. Because Isaac's disability keeps him from seeing the situation properly, it actually may be necessary to direct the blessing to the appropriate recipient through trickery. If Isaac were a different kind of parent and partner, Rebekah might have been able to share with him what she learns from the oracle, that is, the older child's subjugation to the younger (Genesis 25:23), and work *with* Isaac to bless the designated link to the next generation. As this is impossible, Rebekah sees that circumstances demand a ruse. Lest Rebekah seem completely heartless in her dealings with her older son, note that her plan allows the positive relationship between Isaac

---

will be explored in more depth in the discussion of Hannah later in the book.

and Esau to continue unharmed, a relationship that is essential for Esau's well-being. However, the ruse deals a death-blow to the sibling bond.

Mental retardation is not the only disability in Isaac's family. Esau, as we have seen, may suffer from ADHD. The presence of a child with a disability can disrupt a family and lead to marital discord. As noted, there is a striking difference in Isaac and Rebekah's relationship before and after the birth of their children. Rebekah and Isaac's early closeness contrasts sharply with their distance from one another after the birth of their twins, as each parent favors a different child. While Rebekah and Isaac are united in their dislike of Esau's wives (Genesis 26:35), they identify with different children and consequently pursue separate goals (Genesis 25:28). As a result, they create a tense home in which communication is strained and in which the younger son feels he may steal the older child's blessing. In the latter episode (Genesis 27), Rebekah and Esau never speak, and Isaac speaks to Jacob only when Jacob masquerades as Esau. Rebekah and Isaac speak only once. The family members seem almost unable to coexist peacefully.

My Brother's Keeper

Sibling relationships can be strongly affected by the disability of one of the children in a family. It is true that positive relationships between brothers and sisters are possible and can thrive with the right support both from within and outside the family. However, if handled without care, these relationships can result in resentment, jealousy, and anger. Sadly, Jacob and Esau live with a number of problems that have been shown to increase the tension between siblings in families with a disabled family member. Given the limited communication between Isaac and Rebekah following the birth of their sons and given that each favors a different child, it is unlikely that the parents have fostered good feelings between the twins.

Several other conditions probably add to Jacob's poor attitude toward his brother. First, it is hardest for children to accept a sibling with a disability when they are the same sex and close in age.[73] The fact that Jacob and Esau are twins thus puts them at higher risk for conflict. In addition, the greater the number of siblings in the family, the better the psychological adjustment of the non-disabled.[74] Unfortunately, Jacob has no other siblings with whom to share his concerns and struggles. The mother's attitude toward the disabled child also has a significant impact on the siblings' attitude and adjustment.[75] Since Rebekah neither nurtures nor engages with Esau, she does not model for Jacob how to accept a disabled child. Finally, good communication in the home positively affects the non-disabled sibling.[76] Jacob grows up in an uncommunicative household, a place where it is doubtful whether he receives encouragement to treat Esau kindly.

Nurturing the Families that Nurture the Disabled

The Genesis narratives show how important it is to look at the whole family, not just the member with the disability. To help each family member relate appropriately to the disabled individual and deal with his or her special concerns, intervention must focus on the family as a system.[77] For example, siblings of the disabled *might* feel embarrassed, or worry that they will fall victim to the same disability.[78] Thus siblings need guidance and loving care. Parents who wish to help the

---

[73] Lobato, 50.
[74] Ibid., 58-59.
[75] Ibid.
[76] Ibid., 59-60.
[77] For a classic discussion of this concept, see Napier and Whitaker.
[78] Meyer and Vadasy, 8-10.

siblings get along and care about one another first must come to terms with and manage their own guilt, loneliness, and distress. Only then can they concentrate on accepting and loving their disabled child and help their other children cope.

After a long time, Abraham reaches acceptance and can love and care for Isaac.[79] Unfortunately, Jacob and Esau never live in a household that teaches them how to build a relationship. Even many years later, Jacob does not reciprocate Esau's attempts at reconciliation (Genesis 33). Proper modeling and support might have alleviated great pain and allowed Isaac's family to be connected by love and support, rather than separated by hostility.

This chapter focuses on some of the conflicts that can arise in a family when one of its members has special needs and proves that just as the individual with special needs requires sensitive care and nurturing, so too do the non-disabled members of the family. This principle also applies to the parents of a special-needs child. Educators, administrators, and support-service professionals must extend themselves to parents. Professionals can find in God an excellent model of helpful behavior. God supports Sarah even when she is harsh toward Hagar and Ishmael. God engages in personal work with Abraham to transform his perception of Isaac. And when Rebekah is in distress, God delivers a private oracle to her to lend understanding and the strength to carry on. In short, God gives each parent exactly what each needs to cope with their challenges. If educators and other social service professionals follow God's example, they will promote a true partnership between their institutions and the home that will benefit both special-needs children and their families.

---

[79] Although Abraham and Isaac do not speak after the *Akedah*, and while Isaac is remarkably uninvolved in his mother's burial arrangements, Abraham prepares carefully and with great consideration for his son's future.

Joseph and giftedness

The relatively lengthy Joseph cycle in the Book of Genesis tells the rich and dramatic story of Joseph and his family. The text supplies extensive details and yet leaves open many difficult questions. For example, when Joseph is a youth, why does he seem to purposely arouse his brothers' hatred? Why is Joseph's father the only family member who seems to see Joseph in a positive light? How does a character who is initially objectionable manage to shed his irritating conduct, find personal success, and reconcile with his siblings?

Giftedness and Social Isolation

Joseph first appears in the Bible as a spoiled child whose siblings reject him. The text proceeds to follow Joseph through a very challenging and eventful period of growth as he moves from childhood with his family through years of slavery and imprisonment, eventually attaining a high rank in the court of Pharaoh in Egypt. All along, Joseph develops greater sensitivity to others and a deeper understanding of his relationship with God. However, Joseph still has lapses. He deceives his brothers when they come to Egypt in search of food, and financially abuses the starving Egyptians (Genesis 47:13-26).

If we view Joseph as a gifted individual whose exceptional qualities are the source of both his suffering and his success,[80] we discover novel answers to our initial questions. While psychologists and edu-

---

[80] It is noteworthy that several medieval rabbinic commentators interpret the Bible's description of Joseph, "the son of old age to him," to connote a boy who acts older in wisdom and knowledge than is usually expected for one of his years. The rabbis suggest that Joseph possesses the secrets and understanding of someone well beyond his years. (See, e.g., Rashi, Onkelos, Ramban on Gen 37:3).

cators have yet to agree on a definition of giftedness, most accept that it includes superior intellectual, artistic, social, or physical abilities.[81] The Bible introduces Joseph as a motherless young man who is favored by his father Jacob, but despised by his brothers. Jacob loves Joseph best of all because he was born to his favored wife, Rachel, when Jacob was already advanced in years (Genesis 37:3). Jacob's special feelings toward Joseph, which Jacob flaunts with his celebrated gift of the special coat, fans his sons' hatred of their younger brother. To the brothers, the coat is a tipping point beyond which they are unable to see any good in Joseph (Genesis 37:3-4).

In Joseph's first scene, he addresses Jacob and disparages the sons of Jacob's concubines (Genesis 37:2). Since the text does not explain Joseph's motives, it is reasonable to question what he has to gain by telling on his half brothers and why he seems to want to hurt them in the first place. Also, that so many diverse brothers unite to despise Joseph calls into question his ability to form relationships with others. While this distasteful incident can lead us to think poorly of Joseph, we might draw a different conclusion if we view him as a gifted individual. Research has revealed that gifted individuals often experience a fair degree of social isolation. Gifted adults who have been asked to look back on their childhood experiences have suggested that their isolation derived from extreme differences they perceived between themselves and other children, including differences in vocabulary, levels of curiosity, and interests. Some have reported that their isolation lasted into adulthood.[82]

---

[81] Hardman, Drew, and Egan, 512-16.
[82] Subotnik, et al., 42-43.

Giftedness and Problem Solving

After the scene is set and the players are introduced, the narrative focuses on Joseph's dreams (Genesis 37:5-11), which are critical to this reading. Earlier in Genesis, Abraham and Jacob interact with God or heavenly beings in reveries (Genesis 15, 28). Although Joseph is not the first biblical character to have a symbolic dream, he is the first to correctly comprehend its meaning without any divine assistance. Significantly, Joseph's dreams are the first in the Bible in which God does not speak. Rather than theophanies, they are symbolic representations begging to be deciphered. In other words, they are prime opportunities for gifted interpretation.[83] The belief that dreams are meaningful is not new in the context of the Bible, as is evident from Pharaoh and his advisers, who certainly accept it (Genesis 40:8, 41:8). However, Joseph is the first individual in the Bible to recognize that the details in his dreams are symbols, many of which represent future events.

In relation to his dreams, Joseph exhibits two important behaviors characteristic of gifted individuals. The first is the ability to generate original ideas and solutions to problems.[84] Joseph's exceptional intellectual prowess enables him not only to grasp new concepts but also to apply them to his own life. However, Joseph's method of sharing his insights is characteristic of the second behavior often attributed to gifted individuals, a gap between intellectual and emotional maturity. Joseph, in conversation with his brothers, seems insensitive at best, and perhaps even malicious. A good example is when he recounts not one, but two, separate dreams that illustrate his superiority to his brothers. Many gifted children exhibit a marked inconsistency

---

[83] Ages, 48.
[84] Clark, 92.

between their intellectual maturity and their social, emotional, and physical development.[85] Joseph possesses the intellect to comprehend the import of his dreams, but lacks the maturity either to keep the information private, or to share it with a greater degree of sensitivity.

Challenges in Parenting a Gifted Child

Joseph's intellectual gifts stand out in the context of a family comprised of brothers who despise him and a father who adores him. Jacob's special treatment of Joseph causes conflict with Joseph's siblings. Jacob may believe he has good reason to favor Joseph, perhaps because he believes Joseph is exceptional. Unfortunately, however, Jacob is not a model "gifted parent." Not only does Jacob lack the skills to raise such an unusual child, but his job is complicated in a home with multiple wives, concubines, and children. To be fair to Jacob, it is common for parents of gifted children to have doubts about how to handle them or simply to lack the ability to do so. Often, an unprepared parent like Jacob is ambivalent, denying the child's giftedness, while at the same time acting excessively proud of it. Sometimes, the parent is uncertain and anxious about how to properly raise, teach, and ultimately, keep up with, a gifted child.[86] Jacob seems to express a combination of emotions. In one verse he rejects the explosive interpretation of Joseph's second dream (Genesis 37:10), but in the next verse, he "kept the matter in mind" (Genesis 37:11). Here it appears that Jacob appreciates that Joseph's dream is an important prediction about the future, yet denounces it in order to keep peace. The unfortunate dynamics that arise from Joseph's giftedness weigh on his father. Does Jacob believe that Joseph's dreams will come true? Does

---

[85] Ehrlich, 46.
[86] Keirouz, 57-9.

he rebuke his special son for the sake of the brothers, to alleviate their envy? What is Jacob keeping in mind: the dream, or the jealousy of his children? Despite the ambiguity of the text, it is obvious that both Jacob's relationship with his sons and Joseph's relationship with his brothers are highly strained.

Jealous Siblings of Gifted Children

The Bible explicitly states that Joseph's brothers hate and envy him (Genesis 37:4, 8, 11). Joseph's giftedness could account for some of this animosity. Research on the siblings of gifted children has produced mixed results, finding both good and bad relations between gifted individuals and their siblings.[87] However, several factors have been shown to aggravate hostility. For example, when parents label or focus on the gifted child, jealousy among the other siblings increases. In addition, competition, favoritism for the gifted child by one or both parents, and jealousy appear to be greatest when the gifted child is the youngest child.[88] Since Joseph is one of the youngest children and since Jacob singles him out for special treatment, it is reasonable to expect substantial jealousy and discord. The brothers hate Joseph so much that they nearly murder him before selling him to a group of passing traders.

Potential for Success

Joseph's exceptional qualities allow him to rise to the top of every situation. The Bible ascribes Joseph's success to God, although this information is not directly shared with Joseph (Genesis 39:2-3, 21).[89]

---

[87] Chamrad, Robinson, and Janos, 135-45; Colangelo and Brower, 101-103.

[88] Tuttle and Cornell, 408-9

[89] The idea of God as the provider and source of giftedness is hardly restricted to biblical thought.

Potiphar, Pharaoh's chief steward, recognizes that Joseph is incredibly successful and places Joseph in charge of all his household affairs (Genesis 39:4). Here again it is useful to theorize that Joseph is gifted. Two social characteristics of giftedness are a talent for leadership and the ability to solve interpersonal and societal dilemmas.[90] Taking advantage of these precise gifts, Joseph finds success in Potiphar's house, in jail, and in Pharaoh's court. Giftedness may also account for Joseph's habit of persevering in the face of obstacles. In studies, gifted adults have explained that an abiding sense of great possibilities and potential solutions allows them to overcome victimization and defeat when problems arise. Thus, like Joseph, they are especially equipped to take charge.[91]

As much as giftedness may explain Joseph's rise to power in Egypt, it also contributes to his problem in the house of Potiphar (Genesis 39). Potiphar's wife is attracted to Joseph and tries to seduce him many times. On one particular day, she makes an attempt when she and Joseph are alone. After Joseph refuses her advances and escapes her clutches, he accidentally leaves his coat in her hands. He had to have assumed that she would retaliate and that the abandoned coat would give her ammunition to use against him. However, idealism and a sense of justice, two qualities associated with giftedness, guide Joseph's actions.[92] His response to her overtures reflects his principled loyalty to his master and an understanding that submission to his seductress would constitute a sin before God (Genesis 39:8-9).

Joseph is thrown into jail for his alleged indiscretion with Potiphar's wife. Even in this desperate place, he uses his political skills and special insight to achieve a position of influence, and soon is placed in

---

[90] Clark, 99.
[91] Subotnik, et al. 44.
[92] Clark, 95.

charge of the other prisoners (Genesis 39:22). Several years later, his ability to interpret dreams gives Joseph entry into Pharaoh's court, where he rises to second in command (Genesis 41:41ff.). The unique combination of Joseph's giftedness and God's assistance assures Joseph continued success throughout his career in Egypt.

Heightened Emotionality in Gifted Individuals

Joseph's rise to great power sets the stage for the fulfillment of his original dreams. Once he is installed in high office, all that remains is for his brothers to come before him and bow down. Joseph's strong emotional reaction upon seeing his brothers, after years of separation from them, further supports reading Joseph as gifted. The display of intense emotion is a characteristic of gifted individuals.[93] When the brothers arrive in Egypt asking for food, Joseph puts them through a number of trials and terrifying experiences before revealing his identity. Commentators have understood Joseph's treatment of his brothers in Egypt as revenge, as an attempt to educate them, and as an expression of his need to dominate them. Ultimately, it may be his love for and desire to reunite with his father that causes him to stop the charade.[94] Joseph's behavior when he finally reveals his identity to his chastened brothers is extraordinary. Twice he turns away or leaves the room crying (Genesis 42:24; 43:30), and he cries further when he exposes his identity (Genesis 45:1-2, 14-15). While biblical characters often cry upon each others' necks in greeting or parting, this case is unique. The text depicts Joseph holding in his tears, then letting them go, and finally washing his face to hide the fact that he was crying. Note that while Joseph kisses his brothers and weeps, the brothers

---

[93] Clark, 94.
[94] O'Brien, 429-47.

merely talk to him (Genesis 45:15).[95] Only Benjamin, of all 11 of the brothers, weeps together with Joseph (Gen 45:14).

Synthetic Thinking a Gifted Trait

One clue to a new reading of the Joseph story appears when Joseph comforts his brothers and claims that God is responsible for the incredible chain of events that has taken place. With this explanation, Joseph reveals an uncanny understanding of his place in God's scheme, saying: "Do not be pained, and do not let upset be in your eyes that you sold me here for it was to save life that God sent me on before you.... So it was not you that sent me here, but God" (Genesis 45:5-8). It is reasonable to ask how Joseph knows this, for God's actions in this narrative are subtle. God never speaks directly with Joseph, nor, as we have seen, explicitly reveals the divine plan. (Ironically, the narrator explains to the readers that God is with Joseph helping him, but God never explicitly divulges this information to Joseph.) How does Joseph draw his conclusion from the numerous and varied events in his life? Here, his gifted nature is evident[96] in his ability to synthesize the scattered pieces of his experience into a cohesive whole. He sees beyond each individual event in his life and formulates a framework that weaves together the diverse threads. He discerns on his own that there has been a divine plan at work through his whole life, during the adverse, painful moments, and during the moments of joy and triumph. Because Joseph comprehends God's role in his experiences, he can accept his brothers' cruelty and make peace with them.

Unfortunately, Joseph's brothers never seem to share Joseph's vision, nor appreciate the implications of his theological synthesis. Af-

---

[95] Ibid., 447.
[96] Clark, 92.

ter Jacob's death, they are concerned that Joseph's kindness to them has been nothing but a charade for their father's benefit (Genesis 50:15-21). Here again Joseph emphasizes God's part in all that has transpired and assures his brothers of his continuing care for them. Joseph must bear the burden of the gifted individual whose creativity and cognitive abilities can lead to loneliness and misunderstanding.[97] No one else shares his sophisticated perspective on the events he has endured.

"Discovery" and Giftedness

In the Joseph narratives, God acts in the role of the Master Teacher. This time, God's student is the gifted Joseph. Gifted students need teachers who allow them room for discovery. In other words, teachers of the gifted must avoid simply transmitting material and instead, foster conditions that allow students to learn on their own.[98] In essence, this is the teaching model God uses with Joseph. God reveals to Joseph neither the Divine Self, nor the divine plan, but rather, lays out the pieces and gives Joseph the time and space to synthesize the material. Joseph, fearless in the face of the puzzle of his life, is just the student to respond to God's pedagogy.

Where "teaching" Joseph is concerned, God recognizes the importance of educating the "whole person," who is more than a brain or an intellect.[99] To this end, God does not allow Joseph simply to rise meteorically to power. Rather, God leads Joseph along a convoluted trail of experiences that allow him to learn humility, loyalty, and empathy. Only when Joseph's emotional maturity reaches the sophisticated level of his intellectual abilities is he ready to become the leader, and

---

[97] Parkyn, 48.
[98] Lyon, 25.
[99] Lyon, 30-31.

the human being, he was destined to be.

God Modeling Adaptation to the Gifted Child

As we have seen, God seems to have known just how to work with Joseph to facilitate his stellar success. Could Jacob have done a better job with Joseph? If Jacob had understood his son's unique gifts and handled himself properly, he might have prevented, rather than promoted, the sibling rivalry, as well as avoided the events that kept him apart from his beloved son for so long. However, Jacob's life experience does not prepare him for a child like Joseph. That is, since Jacob is used to succeeding primarily with his cunning, he may not be equipped to understand Joseph, who succeeds primarily with his intellect. Perhaps, with proper parenting, some of Joseph's struggles could have been avoided. On the other hand, had Joseph made a better fit with his siblings, he might not have descended to Egypt, risen to greatness, saved his family from starvation and set the stage for the Israelites to be redeemed from Egypt and make their covenant with God.

Joseph's life story leads to a better understanding of the tremendous benefits and great suffering that can accompany exceptional personal and intellectual gifts. This narrative leads us to marvel at Joseph's giftedness, wonder at God's pedagogy, and empathize with Joseph's trials. Notably, God is ever-present in Joseph's life, through his ordeals and successes. God acts as teacher and navigator according to Joseph's needs. God's ability and desire to adapt to Joseph, just like God's ability and desire to adapt to other individuals in the Bible, sets an important standard for us to emulate.

Experiencing the Joseph Cycle as "Gifted Readers"

To some extent, we as readers undergo the same experience as Joseph. Because the narrator reveals and conceals, now giving us information, now withholding it, we must struggle to understand the Joseph story in the same way that he struggles to understand his life. How does Joseph arrive in Egypt? Is he sold to Ishmaelites or stolen by Midianites? As different parts of the text support each thesis, we are forced to attempt to solve the enigma.[100] Similarly, how do we understand Joseph's motives as he juggles concern for his father, love for Benjamin, a desire for vengeance, and a longing to be reunited with his brothers? As Joseph puts different parts of his plan into effect, there is an interplay between his motives. This complexity turns Joseph into a very sophisticated character and requires us to comb the text for answers with great care.

Perhaps we, as readers, are expected to be as gifted as Joseph, building a complete whole from scattered parts without a sure guide to lead the way. The ambiguity of the Joseph story forces us to try and follow Joseph's lead and either analyze the text as "gifted readers," or at least marvel at Joseph's ability to use his gifts. Having to read in this way gives us a window into what giftedness may feel like. While we may not be as successful as Joseph at making sense of events, our efforts may lead to greater empathy for Joseph and a better appreciation for his astounding success.

---

[100] See, e.g. Genesis 37:27-28, 36; 39:1; 40:15; 45:5; Greenstein, "An Equivocal Reading of the Sale of Joseph."

Moses and speech disorders

Moses may be the greatest leader in the Bible. Following his youth in an Egyptian palace and his adulthood as a shepherd in Midian, he assumes leadership of the Israelites at the age of 80. As their leader, Moses is instrumental in bringing the Israelites through their great transition from slaves in Egypt to free people about to enter their future homeland. Moses' accomplishments are incomparable. He helps the Israelites interpret a revelation from God and understand their unique relationship with the Deity. He advocates for the people when God's patience wears thin and encourages them when they lose hope during the trying years in the desert. He wears many hats, acting as prophet, judge, general, parent, nursemaid, and psychologist when circumstances require. At times this heavy load leads Moses to lose faith and give up. Yet, he always resumes the helm with his love and devotion for his God and his people firmly intact.

The Stuttering Orator

Although God believes that Moses is the right person to lead the Israelites, Moses himself doubts that he is the right choice. At least some of Moses' insecurity may derive from his self-image; he perceives himself as "heavy of mouth and heavy of tongue" (Exodus 4:10). Moses knows that speaking both to and for the people is essential for leadership and recognizes that his disability will make it hard for him to fill the position. His difficulty with speech seems to affect his self-perception, his behavior, and his confidence. Given this background, it is reasonable to posit that Moses is a person who stutters.[101]

---

[101] Although the text does not specifically state that Moses stutters, it is fair to say

It seems paradoxical that one of the most ubiquitous voices in the Torah belongs to a man who feels hesitant to speak and may in fact stutter. Three characteristics of Moses' speech point to stuttering: frequent silences, surprisingly short speeches, and the requirement of a spokesperson, Moses' brother Aaron.[102] Moses' trouble with speech appears fairly early in his life, with near-silence during two events when he is a young adult (Exodus 2:11-15). The first incident occurs when Moses goes out to visit with his kinsmen and observes an Egyptian hitting an Israelite. Once Moses is certain that no one is around either to intervene or to witness, he proceeds to kill the Egyptian and hide the body. Surprisingly, not a word is spoken in the entire scene. In the second instance, Moses observes two Israelites fighting. This time Moses tries verbal intervention and asks tersely: "For what reason do you strike your fellow?" In a lengthy speech, one of the Israelites accuses Moses of planning to kill him just as Moses had earlier killed the Egyptian. In contrast with the wordy Israelite, Moses speaks only three words in the whole incident.[103]

Thereafter, Moses flees to Midian, saves Jethro's daughters from

---

that Moses feels his speech disorder impairs his ability to speak clearly and smoothly to others. Stuttering is just such a disorder. It is useful to give a name to Moses' challenge for purposes of discussion and in order to bring pertinent research to bear on it.

[102] This discussion is limited to the first four books of the Torah. The Book of Deuteronomy truly differs from and often contradicts the rest of the Torah in its treatment of law, narrative retellings, and characterizations of God and Israel. Similarly, while Moses is hesitant to speak throughout the first four books, the Book of Deuteronomy presents an entirely opposing characterization of Moses, as the entire book is one long speech. Thus, this chapter deals with Moses as portrayed in the Books of Genesis through Numbers.

[103] I read the next clause in Exodus 2:14 as being one of thought. Moses realizes that the matter of the killing of the Egyptian is known. This works grammatically, since *vayomer* can be used to refer to thought, i.e. one speaking to oneself. (For other examples of this use of the word, see, e.g., 1 Samuel 18:17, 21). This meaning of the verb "*amar*" as thought instead of verbal speech is explained in Rabbi David Kimchi, *Sefer Hashorashim* (Berlin: 1847) 2. This interpretation also works contextually, for it would not be logical for Moses to say these words to his accuser. If we read this clause as being spoken aloud, it still fits with the characterization of Moses as being of very few words, as it contains only three words.

shepherds who are bothering them at a well, marries one of the daughters, and has a son with her. While Moses is the main actor in these dramatic scenes, he never speaks a word (Exodus 2:15-22). His silence is all the more glaring because the words *ki amar*, "for he said," introduce the etiology of the name Gershom, which Moses gives to his son (Exodus 2:22). In the Bible, the phrase "for he said," when used without a direct object, actually means "he thought to himself," or "he thought." Here again, Moses passes through a major turning point in his life without speaking.[104]

Moses is not the first man in the Bible to meet a future wife at a well. It is at wells that Abraham's servant finds Rebekah for Isaac (Genesis 24), and that Jacob first encounters Rachel (Genesis 29). Scholars have classified meetings at wells in the Bible as "type scenes," or scenes that are re-enacted, usually with modifications, in more than one place in a single text.[105] The modifications, no matter how slight, often provide clues to the meaning of each scene. It is crucial to our reading to notice that Moses, unlike Abraham's servant and Jacob, does not speak *at all* at the well. Instead, Moses responds to the threatening shepherds with actions that are conveyed by three strong verbs: "But Moses *rose* up, he *delivered* them, and *gave drink* to their sheep" (Exodus 2:17). In our brief introduction to Moses before he encounters God at the Burning Bush, we find him to be a man of frequent silences and few words who speaks instead with his actions.[106]

---

[104] See previous note.

[105] Alter, *Art of Biblical Narrative*, 54-57.

[106] These traits carry through all of Moses' life. In the frequent episodes of complaint and rebellion by the Israelites in the desert period, Moses repeatedly fails to respond verbally. On the many occasions when Moses actually speaks, he does so after responding silently or physically. He falls on his face, goes directly to God, or, most notably, takes elaborate action after he sees the Golden Calf. (See, e.g., Exodus 5:20; 15:24; 16:2; 32:19-20; Numbers 11:10; 14:5; 16:4; 20:6.)

A very memorable occasion on which Moses uses an extremely small number of words is his beautiful, yet very brief, prayer on Miriam's behalf: "O God, pray, heal her,

Moses' Qualifications

Several of Moses' special characteristics stand out in the famous scene at the Burning Bush. He shows excellent observation skills when he notices the fiery plant and active curiosity when he immediately inspects it. Notably, he does not exhibit a trace of fear. God does not address Moses until God observes him deliberately look at the unique sight: "When YHWH saw that he had turned aside to see, God called to him out of the midst of the bush..." (Exodus 3:3). Had Moses not been perceptive and active, would God have spoken to him? Does God's call to Moses hinge on Moses' interest in the strange phenomenon? We cannot know the answers to these questions. Moses' inquisitive manner, however, in this section of the text contrasts sharply with his repeated attempts to refuse God's commission further on (Exodus 3:11; 4:1,10,13). It is easy to understand Moses' hesitation to return to Egypt. After all, God asks him to go back to a place of great danger and lead a people that have already rejected him (Exodus 2:14). The contrast between Moses' fearlessness and hesitation, however, lends further support to the theory that his speech difficulty explains why he avoids leadership. Moses is not a coward at heart. He does not shy away from new and different experiences. Rather, he is drawn to the unusual. His hesitation about going to Pharaoh, then, is most likely a reaction to his fear of being forced to speak in a public, pressure-filled situation.

Moses' responses to God at the Burning Bush vary in nature and length. First he asks how a person like himself could deliver God's forceful message to Pharaoh, let alone gain access to the king. (Exodus 3:11).[107] Then, Moses requests God's name as a sign of credibility

---

pray!" (Numbers 12:11-12). The brevity is particularly significant since this clearly is a case where Aaron cannot speak for his brother.

[107] On this verse see Rashbam, who spells out Moses' many layers of concern, rang-

(Exodus 3:13), for Moses has a deep concern that neither the Israelites, nor the Egyptians, will believe him (Exodus 4:1). Despite God's reassurance, Moses is not satisfied and finally addresses what seems to be his greatest worry: "Please, my Lord, no man of words am I, not from yesterday, not from the day before, not (even) since you have spoken to your servant, for heavy of mouth and heavy of tongue am I!" (Exodus 4:10). Moses' strong emotion indicates that for him, speaking is troublesome. How can he lead the people and speak to Pharaoh, given his speech impediment? He is both physically and emotionally unable to shoulder this challenge. Why doesn't Moses explain his problem to God in the first place? Some people who stutter do not want to admit that stuttering hinders them. Instead, they offer explanations or excuses for refusing to take on responsibilities or tasks.[108] In this heart-wrenching verse, Moses reveals his anguish and pain. He feels gravely limited because of his disability and can not imagine how he will accomplish the goal God sets out for him. Here, Moses displays a characteristic of some people who stutter and grow to see themselves as stutterers only, to the exclusion of other parts of their identity.[109]

God as Dealer of Disability

After Moses finally bares his soul, God offers a surprising response: "YHWH said to him: Who placed a mouth in human beings or who (is it that) makes one mute or deaf or open-eyed or blind? Is it not I, YHWH? So now, go! I myself will be there with your mouth and will instruct you as to what you are to speak" (Exodus 4:11-12). In this verse, God reveals that Moses' most painful trait, a speech impedi-

---

ing from how he will speak to Pharaoh, to whether he is worthy to address Pharaoh, to what he can say to convince Pharaoh to let his slave labor force simply leave.

[108] Jezer, 83.

[109] Ibid., 16.

ment, is God given! Furthermore, God states that God has chosen Moses to be the people's spokesperson with full knowledge of his speech deficit. Moses' special need in no way disqualifies him from God's service. For the reader, this message may be very uplifting. For Moses, however, the message must be deeply disturbing. Moses must come to terms with the fact that his most intimate relationship will be with the very party who has caused his painful problem.

In a perfect world, Moses' response to God's shocking revelation would have been to accept that God caused the speech impediment and that God would "be with his mouth" (Exodus 4:12). By acquiescing immediately, Moses would have shown faith in God to help him speak and succeed. However, Moses cannot transcend his stuttering and resulting feelings of inadequacy and does not willingly agree to God's plan. Despite God's anger with Moses, God ensures a positive outcome by calling on Aaron, Moses' brother, to be his spokesperson (Exodus 4:14-16). At this point, God responds to Moses' need and provides him with a human "crutch."

Verbal Crutch

Is it a good idea for God to give Moses a fluent spokesperson? Certainly God sees that Moses does not feel able to speak to Pharaoh or the Israelites alone. Today, speech pathologists hold differing opinions about the advantages and disadvantages of electronic devices that help speech-impaired individuals speak more fluently. Marty Jezer, a man who stutters severely, addresses this debate in his book when he discusses Moses:

> God proved to be compassionate by allowing Moses to have his brother Aaron do his public speaking. In court at least I also had an Aaron—a lawyer who

did my talking for me. Yet it was a very strange feeling to be fearlessly confronting what I felt to be injustice while knowing how cowardly I was when it came to stuttering my name. Did Moses feel similarly conflicted? Was the liberator of the Israelites too embarrassed by his stuttering to make a public speech? Alas, the biblical story of Moses is about the liberation of a people from slavery, not the liberation of one person from fear. If it were otherwise, God would have made Moses confront his disability and speak to his people, stutter and all. Moses may be the great liberator of Jewish history, but in giving in to his fear of speaking he's not a role model to this stuttering Jew.[110]

Subsequently, however, Jezer successfully uses an electronic device that helps reduce his stuttering.[111] He reasons that if people with difficulty hearing use hearing aids and people who need crutches use them to walk, people who stutter should use an electronic verbal support.[112] The biblical text expresses a degree of ambivalence that is similar to Jezer's. Throughout Moses' career as a leader, there is tension between God's pushing him to "go it alone" when speaking to the Israelites and God's providing him with a mouthpiece to help him. This tension leads to periods of frustration and anger on Moses' part, as well as to periods of growth and accomplishment. Ultimately, it leads God to prohibit Moses from entering the land of Israel, as we will see.

Once Moses and Aaron become a team, it is not always clear from the narrative whether one or both of them is speaking. In certain

---

[110] Ibid, 35.
[111] An Edinburgh Masker is an electronic device that aids in reducing stuttering by making the person who stutters unable to hear his or her own voice.
[112] Jezer, 224.

places the text says that Moses and Aaron speak together,[113] while elsewhere Moses is the sole speaker.[114] Actually, Moses may not be speaking for himself when the text makes it seem that he is. During the narrative of the plagues, God gives Moses alone a direction to threaten Pharaoh with another plague (Exodus 8:16-19). The text does not mention Aaron. However, reacting to the plague, Pharaoh summons both Moses and Aaron in order to speak to them (Exodus 8: 21). Since the subsequent dialogue appears to take place between Moses and Pharaoh (Exodus 8:22-25), we may wonder why Pharaoh summons Aaron at all. It may be that Aaron is involved in the interchange with Pharaoh in some capacity, perhaps as an interpreter. The evidence suggests that Aaron is his brother's mouthpiece, an interpreter who does the actual speaking, but to whom the words themselves are not attributed.[115]

Speech As Therapy

God never seems to give up encouraging Moses to speak for himself. Soon after Moses and Aaron return to Egypt and begin addressing the Israelites and Pharaoh, God reminds Moses of the covenant and the special relationship with Israel built therein. God instructs Moses to deliver to the Israelites a very hopeful message about the divine plan to take them out of Egypt and bring them to the Promised Land. Although Moses, perhaps uplifted and inspired by God's speech, tries to address the Israelites, they do not listen: "Moshe spoke thus to the

---

[113] See, e.g., Exodus 5:1; 10:3; 16:6; Leviticus 11:1-2; 15:1-2.

[114] See, e.g., Exodus 8:5,21; 14:13; 19:15; 35:1; Leviticus 12:1-2; 16:2.

[115] A good sign of the fluidity appears in Exodus 12:21-28, a section that begins with a statement of various instructions that Moses speaks to the elders, and ends with the confirmation that the elders go and do everything that God had commanded both Moses and Aaron. Although the text begins with a statement about Moses alone, it seems that here, Moses and Aaron are doing the talking together.

Children of Israel. But they did not hearken to Moshe, out of short-ness of spirit and out of hard servitude" (Exodus 6:2-9). Why do the Israelites refuse to pay attention to Moses? Are they too burdened by hard labor to hear any message? Or is it simply too difficult and time-consuming to follow what he is saying? Is his speech so labored and stumbling that they do not have the patience to wait and hear him out? The phrase "*kotser ruach*" "shortness of spirit" can also mean "shortness of breath."[116] If we read this phrase as referring to Moses and not the Israelites, we might infer that the Israelites do not "hear-ken" because it takes such great effort to listen to one who does not speak fluently.

Further support for this reading comes from the next few verses. Moses, who seems to understand that his difficulty with speech is the problem, balks when God directs him to address Pharaoh, claiming that he is "a man of impeded speech" (Exodus 6:12). Since the Isra-elites have just reminded Moses of his speech deficiencies, he refuses to make further attempts with spoken language. God accepts this, and in the next verse returns to give directions to Moses and Aaron together. Later in the same chapter, God tries once more, telling Mo-ses to go and speak directly to Pharaoh. But again, Moses claims that he will fail because of his awkward speech (Exodus 6:29-30). Perhaps God is trying to build up Moses' self-esteem and help him master his disability. God reminds Moses that his charge is not just to speak, but to deliver the divine word, and that God will be with him at all times, providing the necessary words and assistance. In the end, however, Moses sees himself primarily as one who stutters. Unfortunately, research has shown that individuals who incorporate

---

[116] Ramban understands the phrase as "shortness of breath." Rashi, on the other hand, interprets the phrase as "impatience." This, too, fits the model being presented here.

stuttering into their self-concept are more likely to remain stutterers throughout their lives.[117]

Compensation: Singing and Political Theater

Despite his speech problems, Moses manages to lead the Israelites and follow God's commands throughout the years in Egypt and the desert wanderings. Among people who stutter, stuttering may not be present all of the time; its occurrence may depend on the audience or the context. The episodic nature of stuttering, while allowing people who stutter periods of fluency, also results in periods of great uncertainty, since they do not know when they will suddenly begin to stutter.[118] It seems likely that Moses has a degree of comfort with Aaron and with God that he does not feel with the Israelites, and thus is able to speak to Aaron and God with greater ease.[119] He also has periods of apparent fluency, as is evident when he chants the Song of the Sea (Exodus 15). Since it has been shown that stuttering often decreases or disappears when people who stutter act or sing, it should come as no surprise that Moses' speech flows when he performs the Song of the Sea.[120]

On occasion, Moses compensates for his disability with political theater. He holds up his hands in order to win a war (Exodus 17:11), uses his staff while bringing about various miracles, shatters the Ten Commandments (Exodus 32:19), and burns and grinds up the Golden Calf (Exodus 32:20) to express himself where words may fail

---

[117] Berkowitz, Cook, and Haughey, 94.

[118] Blood, 165.

[119] While stress does not cause stuttering, the level of stress in any given situation has an impact on the fluency of an individual who stutters (Jezer, 13-15).

[120] Remarkably, several famous actors and actresses, even some known for their rich voices, stutter. They include James Earl Jones, Bruce Willis, and Marilyn Monroe (Jezer, 239).

him. Marty Jezer describes a similar reliance on social activism and political theater to accomplish his goals. "One theatrical statement was worth, I believed, a thousand words, especially if I had to speak them."[121]

Moses and Frustration

Despite his heroic efforts, Moses' inability to get the Israelites to listen to him and follow God's directions often frustrates and enrages him. From Moses' point of view, the Israelites should accept their faith in God and cease struggling with it. Why, after God has saved them from slavery, given them a constant reminder of the Divine Presence, and met their physical needs, do they persistently rebel? We may speculate about the Israelites' reasons for rebelling, but from Moses' standpoint, the standpoint of one who speaks with God face to face, the Israelites' behavior is incomprehensible. Moses' anger and frustration may also derive from his sense that the Israelites do not listen to him because of his awkward speech.[122] It also may be that he becomes extra frustrated given that he values God's word to such a degree that he puts forth a superhuman effort to deliver it to the Israelites, and yet they don't seem to comprehend what they are missing.

In one episode of anger at the Israelites, Moses describes to God his role as their leader. He compares himself to one who carries the people, just as a parent or nursemaid carries a baby (Numbers 11:10-15). It is significant that Moses does not depict himself as a spokesperson, an intermediary, or some functionary whose work requires speaking. Conversely, when God describes the divine relationship

---

[121] Jezer, 164.

[122] Moses has a strong reaction of anger after the people do not listen to him about the proper amount of manna to gather (Exodus 16:20). Moses could have tried to empathize with the people's fears of starving in the desert that led to their gathering too much manna, but instead reacts with anger.

with Moses, God focuses primarily on speech. God speaks to Moses directly: "mouth to mouth I speak with him" (Numbers 12:8). God's attempts to help develop Moses into a leader who directs with speech also are evident at Mount Sinai, where God engages Moses in verbal communication: "Moshe kept speaking, and God kept answering him in the sound (of a voice)" (Exodus 19:19). Just as God can cause speech difficulties, God can bypass them.

Throughout the desert period, God tries to move Moses to speak for himself. God's efforts peak in Numbers 20, when Moses and Aaron receive instructions to speak to a rock in order to draw out water from it. Previously, Moses had been told to hit a rock to get water (Exodus 17). However, here God raises the ante and challenges Moses to use words, rather than a non-verbal action, in an extremely stressful situation. Unfortunately, Moses fails to speak and strikes the rock. Although Moses disobeys orders, God does not withhold water from the people. However, God prohibits Moses from entering the land of Israel. This seems like an unduly harsh consequence for Moses. Commentators have long puzzled over exactly what makes this act of disobedience so egregious. In the text, God accuses Moses of having failed to show the people God's awesome distinctiveness. Nonetheless, after Moses has worked so hard the punishment seems excessive.[123] Does God punish Moses for flagrant disobedience, before all the people? Does God punish Moses because a leader cannot be successful, or be allowed to continue in his position, once he develops such great intolerance and frustration with his charges?[124] No

---

[123] The Midrash expands on this text with many examples of Moses pleading with God to be able to enter the land, and, occasionally, arguing about his own worthiness, something we would not have seen in the biblical text itself. See, e.g., Midrash Rabbah, Deuteronomy 2:1, 4, 6, 8.

[124] Many have attempted to understand the severity of this "crime" in God's eyes. See, e.g., Kirsch, 304-307.

matter how we interpret the text, the punishment does not seem to fit the crime. After a career of Moses devoting himself to God and the Israelites, it seems cruel to withhold success from him.

New Light on Moses' "Punishment"

Reading the narrative through the lens of special needs allows us to posit a further explanation for the punishment of Moses. Perhaps God, in asking Moses to hit the rock, is giving Moses one last chance to overcome his speech difficulties. Perhaps God had hoped that Moses would recognize that God had chosen him on purpose, stutter and all, and that God would help him say the words. Perhaps God had been hoping that Moses would evolve beyond the need for the kinds of help that had been provided earlier. Moses, with all of his faith and experience of God, does not live up to these hopes. Thus, Moses' failure in the incident with the rock is a terminal failure. When he is unable to use his faculty of speech in a terribly tight spot, he no longer can lead a people that will soon emerge from the desert.

Given this reading, we can view what happens to Moses as a consequence of his behavior rather than a punishment. The case of Elijah provides a strong parallel. When Elijah reaches a level of zeal for God and frustration with the people that makes him an inadequate leader, God tells him to anoint Elisha in his place (1 Kings 19). Elijah is not punished. After all, he is the only prophet who is taken up to heaven in a flaming chariot (2 Kings 2:11). He is simply no longer the right prophet for the historical situation.

Once Israel leaves the desert, God's role changes. God works fewer miracles and no longer is a constant presence. From this point on, the Israelite leader needs to communicate with other peoples and speak to the Israelites in a way that will help them recognize God's often imperceptible presence. The one who will lead the Israelites from the edge of the desert into Canaan must be more comfortable with words than with political theater and dramatic miracles. Because Moses has shown himself unable to fulfill these requirements, God informs him that he is not permitted to enter the Land of Israel.

Reading Moses as a person who stutters illuminates his struggles and strengths and adds to our understanding of his relationship with God. God sympathizes with Moses' disability and tries to help him overcome it. God pushes Moses to appreciate his own self-worth and to trust the Divine Instructor. Perhaps God purposely chooses an individual who stutters for the job of spokesman so that God's success cannot be attributed to charismatic speechmaking by a human.[125]

Whatever God's motives, Moses, with all his strengths and weaknesses, is called on to effect a terribly difficult transition in the life of the Israelite people. Despite his speech disability, Moses is phenomenally successful. He accomplishes all that God asks of him and leads the Israelites from slavery to freedom. Tragically, Moses never seems to find that same freedom for himself.

---

[125] The Bible takes great care to downplay the power of people, lest God seem weak in comparison. This thrust permeates the Book of Judges, where each "judge" possesses a trait that makes him or her an unlikely hero in biblical times: Ehud is left-handed, Jephthah is illegitimate, and Deborah is a woman. In Gideon's time (Judges 7:1ff.) God's directive to Gideon explicitly voices the concern that great human might can make God's strength seem paltry.

Miriam and gender in education

Miriam is a woman of great contradictions. Although she emerges in Exodus as a leader and prophet, she is absent from most of the Exodus narratives. Considering her crucial function in the Israelite community, it is surprising that she appears in only 21 verses in the entire Torah. Although her leadership role during the desert period is never clarified, in a later prophetic text, God recalls sending Moses, Aaron, and Miriam together to bring the Israelites out of Egypt (Micah 6:4). This corrective has led some scholars to believe that the Bible suppresses Miriam's story.[126] Note also that whereas the Bible only briefly mentions that Miriam is the protector of Moses, a joyful song leader, and a beloved member of the community, some rabbinic texts give her credit for the vital function of providing water for the thirsty people in the desert.[127]

The Invisible Woman

Miriam appears in Exodus in several bursts between which she disappears from the narrative. This chapter will begin with an examination of Miriam's alternating appearance and disappearance, prominence and diminution in light of issues of gender. Gender is not ordinarily a concern of special education. However, given that there is often a wide gap between the academic experiences of girls and boys, it is imperative to examine its impact on education. In this chapter, gender is treated as a "special need" because it can affect whether female students in particular receive equal treatment and achieve their

---

[126] See, e.g., Trible, "Bringing Miriam Out of the Shadows."
[127] See, e.g., Rashi on Numbers 12:2.

full potential. "Girls' gender journey must end in self-affirmation and full participation in the educational, economic, and social life of the nation. True educational reform will happen when girls, as well as boys, become all they can be."[128] Therefore, as equal education for both genders is an area of struggle for many students and teachers, it is a fitting topic for this book.

Researchers have gathered a great deal of data on the impact of gender on how students are treated in education settings. In many classrooms, teachers give more attention to boys than girls, and girls who do receive attention can wait longer than boys to get it. Not only do many teachers call on boys more often than girls, but they also interrupt girls more frequently than boys.[129] Of course, this imbalance does not occur in every classroom. Heightened awareness of gender issues has led many teachers to attend equally to all students. However, despite improvements over the years, this continuing problem has both theoretical and practical implications for the education of children. It also affects the experiences of adults in the work force.

Discomfort in Mixed Gender Groups

Reading the Bible through the lens of gender concerns reveals that Miriam is more active in the company of women than in mixed-gender groupings. Further, when she asserts herself around men, she is punished severely (Numbers 12:1-16). Miriam, dynamic in all-female settings and subordinate and passive in co-ed circumstances, exemplifies traditional, female stereotypes.

Miriam first appears in Exodus 2, where she is one of the female characters who saves and protects Moses. While the text does not

---

[128] Jackie Defazio quoted in Orenstein, 277.
[129] Houston, 52.

name these girls and women, each plays a crucial part. Miriam begins her life in tension with the text, which does not even mention her birth. (It must be noted that Aaron's birth is not mentioned as well, while, in contrast, the birth story of Moses is ten verses long.[130]) When the text jumps from the marriage of Moses' parents to the birth of Moses, it simply assumes that Miriam exists and only later refers to his two older siblings, Aaron and Miriam. The concern of the text is Miriam's effect on Moses' life, not her character development.[131]

Nevertheless, Miriam's behavior with regard to Moses says a great deal about her. She is clever, courageous, independent, and loyal to her family when she strategically stations herself along the Nile to observe what will happen to Moses in his tiny vessel (Exodus 2:4). Although the text suggests that Miriam is merely a passive onlooker, she goes on to play a major role in the fate of her infant brother (Exodus 2:7-8).[132] Ironically, just when the reader is supposed to notice Moses, Miriam's actions command attention.

Miriam exhibits great pragmatism and strength of character when she approaches Pharaoh's daughter, who plucks Moses from the Nile. Just a moment after Pharaoh's daughter remarks that the foundling is an Israelite, Miriam boldly offers to find him a wet nurse (Exodus 2:6-7). Here, Miriam is savvy enough to recognize that she is socially inferior to Pharaoh's daughter as well as forward enough to intervene to save her brother. It is Miriam who seems to suggest that Pharaoh's daughter raise Moses as her own son. This is not to say that Miriam dupes Pharaoh's daughter, or forces her decision, for the Egyptian already knows the baby is an Israelite. Rather, Miriam's quick thinking and gutsy proposal allow Moses to be returned to the care of their

---

[130] Exodus 2:1-10.
[131] Trible, "Bringing Miriam Out of the Shadows," 167-68.
[132] Ibid., 168.

birth mother, Yocheved. Once Miriam brings Yocheved into the picture, Yocheved begins to nurse Moses. Since Yocheved probably nurses Moses for three years or more, Miriam should receive credit for reuniting mother and son for this formative period of his life.

Miriam takes the lead whenever the rest of the characters in the scene are women. (The only male at the Nile is the infant Moses, who is too unformed as a character to dominate the action. Moses' father disappears from the narrative immediately after marrying Moses' mother.) Cheryl Exum has focused on this issue in her discussion of gender in the Bible, noting as we have, that several, mostly unnamed, women together save Moses. This reduces each woman's individual impact. According to Exum, this is probably deliberate, as the biblical text represents the traditional point of view of a patriarchal society with its general suspicion of powerful women. The biblical narrator, expressing this patriarchal fear of women's power, would not have tolerated a story in which a woman is responsible for the rescue of Moses; such a woman would have been too capable or too strong, and thus, a threat to the status quo.[133]

To save Moses, the women cooperate and network. These two social strategies are frequently associated with women.[134] The women in the narrative seem to ignore the differences between their social classes. Though Pharaoh's daughter is far more powerful and higher on the social ladder than the other women, each one of them plays her part to help save the baby. Yocheved hides Moses and then places him in the reeds. Miriam watches him and arranges the transfer to Pharaoh's daughter. Pharaoh's daughter treats the Israelite infant as if he were her own and her maidens protect her secret. Miriam seems

---

[133] Exum, "Second Thoughts about Secondary Characters," 83.

[134] See, e.g., the writings of Deborah Tannen, such as *You Just Don't Understand: Women and Men in Conversation.* New York: Morrow, 1998.

comfortable with cooperating and participates with ingenuity.

Who's the Songwriter in the Family?

Miriam next appears after the Israelites cross the Sea of Reeds. This dramatic crossing helps the people comprehend God's power and develop faith and trust in God and Moses. Through the beautiful poetry of the Song of the Sea, which Moses and the Israelites sing once they reach safety, they express their understanding of God's nature and power (Exodus 15:1-19). Immediately following the song, Miriam and the women act: "Now Miriam the prophetess, Aaron's sister, took a timbrel in her hand, and all the women went out after her, with timbrels and with dancing. Miriam chanted to them: 'Sing to YHWH, for God has triumphed, yes triumphed, the horse and its charioteer God flung into the sea!'" (Exodus 15:20-21). The women's chant repeats the first verse of the song nearly verbatim. The women's refrain raises many questions. Why does the text call Miriam Aaron's sister? Does Miriam lead just the women or the men as well?[135] Why does her song merely repeat the beginning of the song Moses sang?[136]

Some scholars suggest that Miriam may be the actual author and leader of the Song of the Sea.[137] If this is the case, why doesn't the text say so? It may be that the text was redacted from a patriarchal viewpoint so that Miriam's political role was subverted or suppressed.[138] It may be that the text is using analepsis, a technique of temporarily withholding information so that it may be introduced later. If this is the case, Miriam actually sings at the beginning of the Song of

---

[135] Note the use of the third person plural masculine possessive pronoun *lahem*.

[136] We are not the first generation to be struck by the absence of Miriam's song. The reworking of the Pentateuch found in Qumran (4QRP) added a poetic section which could very well have been intended as the Song of Miriam (Attridge, 268-71).

[137] See, i.e., Janzen.

[138] Trible, "Bringing Miriam Out of the Shadows," 172.

the Sea, but does not receive credit until further on.[139] According to both of these views, Miriam could be leading the song either with, or in place of, Moses. It has even been suggested that her short, poetic song, comprising the first few lines about God's power and heroism, may be the original kernel of the Song of the Sea.[140] In any reading of the Song of the Sea, Miriam clearly is a leader in the community, at least among the women. She is the first woman whom the Bible calls a prophetess. Her designation as the sister of Aaron, with no mention of Moses, may indicate that although neither is on Moses' level,[141] her stature is equal to Aaron's (Exodus 15:20).

Some scholars have pointed out the literary artistry in the position of Miriam's song in the text, at the conclusion of the scene at the sea. Her song marks the end of the deliverance from Egypt. Thus, Miriam bookends the redemption of the Israelites, appearing in the beginning as the protector of Moses, and at the conclusion as the prophetess of deliverance. The narrative starts and finishes with the same woman at times enabling, at times watching, and at times celebrating God's power.[142]

The location of Miriam's song in the Biblical text has additional ramifications. Notice that the clever Miriam who appears at the beginning disappears from the text. Whereas among women Miriam has great gumption and quick intelligence, with men she more or less repeats what they have said. The change in Miriam parallels findings in gender education: Women in mixed groups, even on the postsecondary level, are less likely to speak assertively than when they are

---

[139] Janzen, 198.

[140] Goitein, 7.

[141] This is not a gender issue. The Torah makes exceedingly clear that no other human being can be on the same level as Moses in his or her relationship with God (Deuteronomy 34:10).

[142] Fox (1995), 336.

MIRIAM AND GENDER IN EDUCATION

with women alone.[143] The song Miriam might have sung only in the presence of women would have been very different from the song as it stands in Exodus 15.

Miriam: The Victim

Miriam's final scene before her death in the desert is laced with tension between Miriam and Aaron on one side and Moses on the other. At the ambiguous beginning of Numbers 12, Miriam and Aaron seem to speak against Moses because of his Cushite wife. It is difficult to tell whether they are referring to Moses' Midianite wife, Tzipporah, or to another woman whom Moses may have married subsequently. No matter to whom they refer, authority is the core of their mini-rebellion, for Miriam and Aaron go on to claim that God speaks through them as well as through Moses. God reacts swiftly to quell their hubris, making it completely clear that no other human can achieve Moses' level of inspiration and connection with the Divine. After God punishes Miriam with leprosy[144] and Aaron has Moses pray for healing on her behalf, God changes her sentence to banishment from the desert camp for a week.[145]

Although Miriam and Aaron speak their words of rebellion together, the text cites Miriam first: "Now Miriam spoke, and Aaron, against Moses on account of the Cushite wife that he had taken-in-marriage" (Numbers 12:1). However, when God angrily calls to them in response, the sequence of their names changes: "And YHWH said suddenly to Moses, to Aaron, and to Miriam. . ." (Numbers 12:4). An analysis of this verse's structure supports this reading. Each proper

---

[143] Houston, 52-53.

[144] For an analysis of leprosy as a punishment for specifically challenging divine or prophetic authority, see Abrams, "*Metsora(at) KaShaleg*."

[145] Milgrom, 98.

name occurs separately with a preposition preceding it. The grammar isolates the siblings from one another and underlines that each is an individual. At this stage, Aaron's name precedes Miriam's. This occurs again when God calls only Aaron and Miriam for rebuke and punishment: "And YHWH descended in a column of cloud and stood at the entrance to the tent; He called out: Aharon and Miryam" (Numbers 12:5). Thus in a short span of verses, the text eradicates the confidence and certainty that Miriam has when the chapter opens.

While we may applaud Miriam's self-assuredness, we cannot admire her goals in this scene. Both God and the narrator emphasize that Moses, despite his famed modesty, is head and shoulders above Miriam and Aaron. This is one reason why generation after generation of readers has found it surprising that God's anger with Miriam and Aaron (Numbers 12:9) is followed by God's punishment of Miriam alone. Why does Aaron escape punishment? Some Bible scholars have asserted that Aaron is spared because he is the High Priest; a bout of leprosy would have prevented him from carrying out his priestly functions, including offering sacrifices.[146] It is also possible that Aaron's punishment is the demoralizing realization that he cannot help Miriam, but that he must ask his more powerful brother to pray on her behalf. Perhaps Miriam's gender can explain her punishment. If so, Miriam's punishment reflects that assertive women are more likely to be put down than assertive men.[147] While it may seem that God treats Miriam unfairly, note that God's swift and harsh action is not imitated in the human realm. On the contrary, the people show their continued love and respect for Miriam by waiting for her while she sits outside the camp. They do not budge until she re-enters the community.

[146] Fox (1995), 716.
[147] Graetz, 232-33.

Miriam's plight seems to mirror the experiences of girls in the classroom. Often, their passivity is reinforced and their assertiveness is squelched.[148] Although Miriam conducts herself no differently from Aaron, she, not her brother, is publicly punished. From a gender perspective, because the punishment involves separation and isolation, it seems especially harsh. For Miriam, who seems to thrive on connections with other women, the isolation may be harder to bear than the leprosy.

Seeking Universal Validation

When we view Miriam through the lens of the special concerns we should have for girls and women in education settings, we see that her character is most sharply drawn and actualized in single-sex, all-female groupings. Women seem to value her passion and dynamism. Among men, these qualities bring her severe trouble. The Miriam who waits by the Nile and who joyfully dances and sings at the Sea is a woman we would like to know better. Unfortunately, we can only speculate about the extent of her influence. Perhaps Miriam's leadership sets an example for the daughters of Zelophehad and gives them the courage to go before Moses and Elazar with their case (Numbers 27). Perhaps it is Moses' understanding and appreciation of his sister that leads him to take the women's query to God without question or hesitation. While Miriam's life may have ended quietly and without the recognition she deserved, it is possible to claim that she laid the groundwork for future generations of women to step up and raise their voices.

---

[148] Houston, 52.

Samson and conduct disorders

In the period of the Judges, a steady stream of leaders arises to save Israel from oppression. During the time of the Philistine scourge, a man named Samson emerges as judge in Israel. His often boorish, unsophisticated behavior sets him apart from the other leaders of his era. Samson also differs from them because he fights the enemies of Israel on his own rather than lead the Israelites in battle. Despite Samson's strange, often violent conduct and lonely way of life, he eventually achieves a victory for Israel. Remarkably, the text states and later reiterates that God is with Samson and is the source of his success. The contrast between Samson's close relationship with God and his coarse personality, in addition to the many oddities of plot, character, and style have baffled many Bible scholars. One has even called the narrative "a large riddle."[149]

Samson is an exceedingly troubled individual who engages in dangerous, risky behavior and causes untold damage and pain to himself and others. Perhaps one way to explain Samson is to view him as a person with a conduct disorder.[150] A conduct disorder is characterized by a repetitive or persistent pattern of behavior violating the basic rights of others or major age-appropriate norms or rules.[151] It includes aggression to people and animals, destruction of property, deceitful-

---

[149] Greenstein (1981), 237-260.

[150] Dr. Eric Altschuler and his colleagues at the University of California at San Diego have also linked Samson with antisocial personality disorder. See, e.g. University of California, San Diego (2001, February 26). "Biblical Hero Samson May Have Been Sociopath As Well As Strongman, According To New Research." ScienceDaily. Retrieved May 21, 2011, from http://www.sciencedaily.com/releases/2001/02/010223081053.htm. Also, I thank Dr. Barbara Bard for her insights into Samson's character.

[151] Forness, et al., 306-12.

ness, and rule breaking.[152] Further symptoms may include bullying, initiating fights, using weapons, destroying property, setting fires, lying, and stealing.[153] Over the course of his life, Samson exhibits nearly all of these behaviors.

Following Samson's birth, his first independent act occurs when he informs his parents that he wishes to marry a Philistine woman (Judges 14:2). We form our initial impression of the adult Samson when he strays from societal norms and makes an inappropriate demand. His parents respond that it would be far more acceptable for him to ask for an Israelite woman (Judges 14:3). Samson does not seem bothered by his parents' concern. Although he cannot explain his attraction to the Philistine woman, he insists that she is the right wife. This flagrant violation of social standards is in keeping with the characteristics of a conduct disorder. Since Samson never shows affection or concern for his betrothed, it seems unlikely that he feels "true love" for her. In keeping with the symptoms of having a conduct disorder, he shows a lack of empathy.

In short order, Samson begins an eventful journey that is filled with aggression toward both animals and people. At the outset, Samson, without any weaponry, tears apart a lion that roars at him (Judges 14:5-6). Later in the journey, Samson continues his odd, alarming behavior when he purposely returns to see the remains of the lion (Judges 14:8). Samson shows his impulsiveness when he kills the lion. In returning to the carcass and consuming the honey from the site, he demonstrates an attraction to violence and death. Behaviors like Samson's fit the profile of some people with conduct disorders.

---

[152] Sommers-Flanagan and Sommers-Flanagan, 189.
[153] Forness, 306.

Not a Great Friend

Samson follows violence toward an animal with far more severe violence toward men (Judges 14:10-19). During his ensuing wedding feast he challenges his guests to figure out a riddle. He promises to reward them with tunics and other garments if they correctly guess the answer; if they fail, they must give him the same prize. The puzzled men, unable to solve the riddle, threaten Samson's new wife and demand the answer. She in turn nags Samson throughout the week-long feast until she wears down his patience and he gives her the solution.

The riddle episode contains several crucial details. Note first that Samson's parents assign him "friends" during his wedding feast (Judges 14:11). He neither brings his own friends to the wedding, nor seems to belong to a social group. Only Samson's parents accompany him to his wedding, and only they provide "companions" with whom he can celebrate. Not only does Samson seem to lack friendships, but he seems to lack an intimate, loving relationship with his wife. During the riddle narrative, Samson's "friends" from the wedding put his wife in a terrible bind. They force her to choose between violence to herself and her family on the one hand, and disloyalty to her new husband on the other. In the end, his wife decides to save her family and puts their well-being above her relationship with Samson.

Poor Marital Bond

A second key detail is that Samson seems to be more loyal to his parents than to his wife. When she pushes him to reveal the answer to the riddle, he exclaims, "I haven't even told my father and my mother; shall I tell you?" (Judges 14:16). His loyalty to his parents comes first. This primacy of the parent-child relationship over the spousal relationship contradicts the normative model of marriage described in Genesis: "Hence a man leaves his father and mother and clings to his wife, so that they become one flesh" (2:24). The wife's decision to side with her family is understandable. If she remains loyal to Samson, her family will suffer violence, while if she betrays Samson, he will suffer only a financial loss. However, Samson's lack of connection to his wife makes less sense. Some of his interpersonal problems may result from a conduct disorder. Researchers have observed that children with conduct disorders have difficulty forming strong relationships because they often lack sensitivity to the perspective of others and tend to show low levels of empathy, if they show any at all.[154] This may explain why Samson has no friends to bring to his wedding and why there exists a less than ideal relationship between the new bride and groom.

In the same scene, Samson demonstrates further impulsiveness as well as an inability to grasp the meaning of long-term consequences. From the moment his wife begins to nag him for the answer to the riddle, Samson is very hesitant to share the solution with her. He probably questions her loyalty, which may explain why he withstands her relentless harassment for six days (Judges 14:16-17). It is not until the final day of the wedding festivities that he tells her what she wants to know. Perhaps he cannot tolerate even one more moment of intense harassment by his spouse. Since Samson is suspicious of her, and since he has already outlasted her nagging for the better part of the wedding week, we would expect him to put up with the discomfort just a little longer and win his bet. Instead, he gives in on the last day, when he is tantalizingly close to winning out. He cannot tolerate a little more short-term pain for significant long-term gain.

---

[154] Matthys, 523.

Samson's Violent Nature

Having lost the bet, Samson pays the promised prize. However, he does this by killing thirty innocent men, stripping them of their clothes, and delivering the garments to the men of the town. It is significant that Samson murders the men after the spirit of God comes upon him (Judges 14:19). Unlike the majority of the leaders in the Book of Judges, who harness God's aid in their battles against oppressive enemies of the nation, Samson, also a leader designated by God, relies on God's spirit to give him the strength to kill innocent people in order to pay off a personal bet.

The following incident is simultaneously gory and sad. It begins with Samson's attempt to follow societal norms and show remorse for having left the wedding feast immediately after the riddle fiasco (Judges 14:19). He visits his wife with a gift for her family in hand. Understandably, given the tragic wedding, her family turns him away (Judges 15:1). Then Samson learns that his erstwhile father-in-law has given his daughter to another man, either to show he rejected Samson and his violence, or because he assumed that when Samson left the wedding, he left for good. Samson's response is immediate and violent. He ties torches to the tails of pairs of foxes and sets them loose on the Philistines' crops and fields (Judges 15:4-5). In this horrifying episode, Samson exhibits many of the signs that indicate a conduct disorder, including setting destructive fires, abusing animals, and wrecking property. He responds to his father-in-law's insult with savagery and vandalism aimed at the entire community and does not seem to comprehend that his behavior is unreasonable. When his father-in-law tries to explain why he gave his daughter away and offers a solution, Samson states: "Now the Philistines can have no claim against me for the harm I shall do them" (Judges 15:3), as if mass destruction were an appropriate response to an insult! Samson follows the arson with a battle against the Philistine people (Judges 15:8). A symptom of conduct disorder is a difficulty behaving according to social norms,[155] and it is precisely this symptom that Samson exhibits in this section of the text.

Samson's activities continue in a running narrative of killing and property destruction. When he takes up with Delilah, a woman from the Wadi Sorek, he begins a pattern of lying as well. Despite her many efforts to uncover the truth about his superhuman strength, he repeatedly deceives her about it (Judges 16:6-14). Finally, after he succumbs to her pressure, the Philistines capture him (Judges 16:16-21). As his dying act, he tears down their temple, causing more destruction and death than he had in his lifetime (Judges 16:28-30). By this point in the narrative, it becomes clear that Samson's actions fall into a relentless, life-long pattern of behavior that is consistent with conduct disorders.

To be diagnosed with a conduct disorder, an individual need exhibit only three of the anti-social or problematic behaviors from the long list we have examined.[156] Samson, however, far exceeds the minimum. Moreover, the severity, variety, and frequency of his disturbing behaviors point to a particularly severe conduct disorder. "The best predictors of continuity of conduct disorders are age of onset, the variety of anti-social acts, frequency, problem behavior in multiple settings and severity."[157] Throughout his life, Samson perpetrates destructive and brutal acts, both provoked and unprovoked, in many different settings, against animals and people, against groups small and large.[158] Unfortunately, there are few lulls in the narrative between his

[155] Kamps and Tankersley, 45.
[156] Hardman, Drew, and Egan, 224.
[157] Clarizio, 262.
[158] Arllen, Gable, and Hendrickson, 19.

maladaptive episodes. Samson's biography is a litany of destruction.

Indulgent and Negligent Parenting

The role of Samson's parents is fundamental to this discussion. Given that their only important accomplishment seems to be the birth of Samson, they are surprisingly prominent in the narrative. Samson's elaborate birth story involves a detailed annunciation to both parents (Judges 13). This is a rare phenomenon in the Bible; in most cases, only one of the parents receives the annunciation.[159] During the two-stage annunciation of Samson, an angel repeats the announcement with slight changes the second time. The annunciation involves notice of the upcoming birth, instructions for how to raise Samson (including a special diet and a prohibition against cutting his hair), and a prediction that he will someday save the Israelites. The annunciation scene stands out because of the parents' mix of fear, disbelief, and foolishness. They ask to have the annunciation repeated, misunderstand parts of the message, struggle to recognize that their visitor is an angel, and then worry that they will die because they have encountered a divine being.[160]

A comparison of Samson's birth announcement with other birth announcements in the Bible, such as the announcements made to Abraham and Sarah, Hagar, and Hannah, sheds light on our hypothesis about Samson. Abraham, Sarah, Hagar, and Hannah quickly recognize the importance of the divine annunciation. Hagar so deeply appreciates the importance of the annunciation of Ishmael that she

---

[159] See, e.g., the annunciation to Hagar (Genesis 16:7-14), to Abraham (Genesis 18:1-15), and to the Shunamite woman (2 Kings 4:15-17). While Sarah hears about Isaac's upcoming birth at the same time as Abraham, she only learns the information by eavesdropping on the annunciation.

[160] For more on Samson's parents' unusual response to the annunciation, see Exum, *Fragmented Women*, 61-65, and Amit, 148-50.

willingly returns to a very difficult living situation with Sarah, who resents her (Genesis 16:7-13). Because Abraham (Genesis 17) understands the meaning of the forthcoming birth of Isaac, he protests to God that he is satisfied with Ishmael, the son he already has, and does not need another son. Although both Abraham and Sarah react to God's promise of a child with laughter, perhaps indicating some initial doubt and disbelief, God's rebuke quickly sobers them (Genesis 17:17-22; 18:12-15). When Hannah learns that her prayers for a child will be answered, she feels comforted and becomes tranquil (1 Samuel 1:18). Samson's parents' response, unlike the others, descends into a panic of foolish questions, comments, and actions.

As the narrative progresses, Samson's mother and father repeatedly show that they are inadequate parents. When Samson asks for a Philistine woman, they question him but do not deny his request. Even if they do not have the power to refuse him, the text is silent about any hard feelings they may harbor about Samson's choice of wife. Contrast this, for example, with the negativity that Isaac and Rebekah express toward Esau's Hittite wives (Genesis 26:34). Although Isaac and Rebekah are ultimately unable to control Esau's choice of brides, they do not hide their dissatisfaction with his selections.

At the same time, there seems to be unusual intimacy between Samson and his parents. He makes it clear that he feels closer to them than to his wife (Judges 14:16). Samson's exceptionally strong bond with his parents may stem from being a Nazirite, as the unusual lifestyle might isolate him and make it difficult for him to form relationships with peers. While we can only speculate why Samson is close with his parents, the fact is that the Samson narrative provides a striking picture of parental influence. Much of the literature on conduct disorders discusses the role of the parents. Studies have shown that there is a "direct relationship between the styles of interaction in a family and the behavior problems of the children. Coercive, harsh, and inconsistent disciplinary practices, along with poor monitoring and supervision," significantly affect children's levels of aggression. Other dysfunctional parenting styles, such as giving little positive reinforcement and the inability to model good social behavior, problem-solving, or communication skills can contribute to conduct disorders in children. "Parents of children at risk for conduct disorders may lack the social skills their children will need to negotiate typical adult and peer interactions." [161]

These studies support our observations about Samson's parents. Uncomprehending and clumsy in the annunciation scene, Samson's parents cannot manage this crucial situation. They seem to parent by indulging Samson's wishes and desires and by following the rigid restrictions for raising a Nazirite. Thus, the literature's emphasis on the effect of parents on conduct disorders in children fits very well with the parenting Samson receives and with the theory that he has this special need.

God's Strange Choice

God plays a disturbing part in the Samson narrative. The text makes very clear that God works *through* Samson's unusual and inappropriate behavior in order to terrorize the Philistines (See, e.g., Judges 14:4, 6, 19; 16:28). It even appears that God is responsible for some of Samson's unacceptable conduct, such as his desire to wed a Philistine. Although the text does not state that God makes Samson act out, there is no question that it is God who has given Samson his

---

[161] Kaiser and Hester, 121-22.

unusual strength,[162] who determines that Samson will be a hero before Samson's birth, and who supports Samson even when he is cruel! Although Samson's behavior, with its brutality and disregard for life and property is not what we generally expect from a biblical leader, we must acknowledge that Samson is an agent of God's will and plan. The Samson text demonstrates that in the Bible, God chooses a wide variety of characters as messengers of the divine word and will.

---

[162] See, e.g., Judges 14:6,19.

Mephiboshet and Jacob: dealing with physical disabilities

Two biblical characters struggle with physical disability: Jacob and Mephiboshet, son of Jonathan and grandson of King Saul. Jacob is wounded during his struggle with an angel right before his reunion meeting with Esau. Mephiboshet sustains an injury which causes him to lose the use of his legs on the day that both his father and grandfather die. Jacob becomes an individual who struggles with pain and a limp. Mephiboshet has to find a way to thrive and survive with paralysis. Both men's lives are deeply influenced by their disabilities.

Jacob

In anticipation of his reunion with Esau, Jacob makes elaborate preparations: he separates his camp, he sends generous gifts to Esau, and he pleads with God for help (Genesis 32). The night before the expected meeting, Jacob is left alone and he meets a "man" with whom he struggles all night. When the man realizes that he cannot prevail over Jacob, he hurts Jacob in the leg, dooming Jacob to a permanent limp. Despite the injury, however, Jacob perseveres in the fight, understanding that his foe is more than what he seems, and insists upon the bestowal of a blessing before allowing the being to take his leave. Jacob is blessed with a new name and told that henceforward he will be known as Israel, Striver with God. The reader anticipates that Jacob might continue to act in a strong, determined way to live up to his new name. However, this is not entirely how Jacob reacts after his injury.

Jacob successfully manages the encounter with his brother the very next day. Esau is loving and caring. He asks for them to reconnect: to travel and live together. Jacob responds that it is not possible for him to accompany Esau on their travels because Jacob's family will slow Esau down (Genesis 33:13-14). Although we know that Jacob has little desire to travel with Esau, it is perhaps also true that Jacob can no longer keep up with Esau's pace even if he wants to. Rather than admit his new pain and disability, Jacob prefers to claim that he needs to move slowly because of his children and flocks. Jacob hides his pain, and goes his own way.

In the next chapter, however, Jacob seems far more subdued than his new name might suggest. When Jacob's daughter, Dinah, is raped, a devastating affront not only to Dinah, but to the honor of her whole family, Jacob refuses to take any stand without his sons present (Genesis 34:5). He seems weak and nervous, and scared of his neighbors. When two of his sons react violently, killing all the men of the village where Dinah's rapist lived, and where Dinah was being held, Jacob reacts to them in anger. While one can imagine Jacob's very mixed emotions at this moment, relief that his daughter is home safe, anger that his sons reacted so violently, questioning of his sons' moral states, his only response is one of fear that now he is in danger among his neighbors (Genesis 34:30).

A similar dynamic can be seen early in the Joseph story, when Jacob does not stand up to his sons following the news of Joseph's "death." There are many possible readings of the Joseph story, and of Jacob's recognition, or lack thereof, of his sons' intense anger and hatred of Joseph. Jacob's reaction to the news of Joseph's death, however, is quite striking, regardless of his understanding of the family dynamic. When the brothers approach Jacob, and show him Joseph's bloody tunic, Jacob immediately fills in the story for them. "He said: 'My son's coat. An evil beast ate him. Joseph has been totally torn apart'" (Genesis 37:33). Jacob then continues to tear his own garment and begin an elaborate time of mourning. It is striking that he never considers that perhaps Joseph is lying hurt, but still alive. Why does he not consider that perhaps they should try to retrieve the body to allow for a proper burial? Rather, he allows the brothers' ruse to stand. Is it possible that Jacob "knows" on some level that his sons are responsible in some way for Joseph's disappearance, and is avoiding the confrontation? Once again, Jacob presents as afraid, weak, and unwilling to face conflict. Wounded Jacob now seems a nervous, vulnerable man, who deals with his disability and his pain, and who has less faith in his ability to take charge in situations.

This is a very different Jacob than the one who made sure that he got exactly what he wanted, whether that meant engaging in trickery, cleverness, or hard work. Jacob had been the younger son that managed to leave home with the birthright and the blessing. Jacob was the foreigner who entered Laban's house with nothing, and left with a large family and substantial cattle. Jacob was willing to negotiate with God to ask for protection and success. While it is not surprising that Jacob should go through a personality change after wrestling with a divine being, how interesting that he became more fearful, more nervous, more concerned with being vulnerable, after his success at that struggle.

Mephiboshet

From birth, Mephiboshet, son of Jonathan and grandson of King Saul, is treated like a future king. However, in his fifth year, his life takes a dramatic turn in a single day (2 Samuel 4:4). That day, his father and grandfather both die in battle. When the sad news reaches the royal household, Mephiboshet's nurse grabs him to flee with him to safety. During the hasty flight, Mephiboshet falls and loses the use of both legs. In less than 24 hours, Mephiboshet is transformed from healthy crown prince into a physically disabled orphan with a dangerous, uncertain future.

The Emphasis on Disability

It is not entirely clear how these losses affect Mephiboshet, but certain hints present themselves as he makes his first appearances in the text: "Jonathan son of Saul had a son whose feet were crippled. He was five years old when news came from Jezreel about Saul and Jonathan, and his nurse picked him up and fled. In her haste to flee, he fell and became lame and his name was Mephiboshet" (2 Samuel 4:4). The structure of the verse highlights Mephiboshet's suffering. It begins with Mephiboshet's connection to both his father and grandfather and the fact that they have died. Mephiboshet's physical disability follows, and is mentioned a second time near the end of the verse.[163] However, his name is not mentioned until the end of the verse, as if it were far less important than his personal struggles. The text seems determined to define Mephiboshet by his disability. His name, which contains the word *"boshet,"* meaning "shame," has a negative valence.[164] Not only is his name one of shame, but he is the "crippled one," and not even "Mephiboshet."

---

[163] One personal account of a woman with a physical disability is remarkably similar to the case of Mephiboshet. Her family had an accident during which her father died, her mother was badly hurt, and she herself became paralyzed from the waist down. She claimed that the loss of her father was much harder to bear than the loss of her legs. Perhaps Mephiboshet felt similarly, which explains the order of his introduction--first his relations, then his legs (Krementz, 65-67).

[164] This negative appellation is used, as opposed to the name "Meribaal" in 2 Samuel 4:4. See the discussion in McCarter, 124-25.

This image of Mephiboshet as physically disabled follows him into adulthood. David, having made a vow of everlasting friendship to Jonathan seeks to find and help Jonathan's descendants. He learns about Mephiboshet through Ziba, a servant of Saul's house. In this section of the narrative, there is an important description of Mephiboshet: "There is still a son of Jonathan whose feet are crippled" (2 Samuel 9:3). Here too, the text plays up his disability. There are no other details about Mephiboshet; even his name is absent. After David meets with Mephiboshet and grants him privileges and land, the section concludes with this reference to Mephiboshet: "he was lame in both feet" (2 Samuel 9:13). We are never allowed, not even for a moment, to forget that Mephiboshet has a physical disability.

Keeping Faith with Jonathan's Child?

David's grand gesture toward Mephiboshet begins an ambiguous and difficult relationship. On the surface, David seems eager to fulfill his vow to Jonathan through kindness to Jonathan's son. However, there is reason to question David's motives. Although David's words often express deep feeling for others, his actions are politically expedient.[165] If he is really motivated by loyalty to Jonathan, why does he wait until this point in the narrative to fulfill his pledge of friendship? Strategically, it is especially prudent for David to keep tabs on Saul's descendants and ward off any rebellion at this critical time in his young reign. Perhaps David felt that he had to secure his power base before approaching Saul's descendants. However we understand David's motives, it is worth noting that the differences between the Davidic House and the House of Saul are indicated in textual descriptions of David and his family, with a focus on beauty and physi-

[165] See, e.g., David's responses to the deaths of Saul and Jonathan (2 Samuel 1:11-27), Avner (2 Samuel 3:31-39), and Ishboshet (2 Samuel 4:9-12).

cal abilities, while Saul's house is described in terms of a disabled grandson, and a barren daughter.[166]

He says/He says

Two scenes reinforce the ambiguity of David's motives. At the time of his son Absalom's rebellion, David flees Jerusalem with his entourage. Along the way he has several encounters with various supporters, one of whom is Ziba, Mephiboshet's servant and aide (2 Samuel 16:1-4). When David asks about Mephiboshet, Ziba tells him that Mephiboshet has remained in Jerusalem, where he is taking advantage of David's absence and weakness to regain the kingship. David grants all Mephiboshet's land to the servant, Ziba. Subsequently, when David returns to Jerusalem, Mephiboshet, looking unkempt, meets him with expressions of love and devotion (2 Samuel 19:25-31). Mephiboshet sorrowfully explains that he was unable to greet David as he fled from Jerusalem because Ziba deceived him and left him behind. After hearing this, David changes his plan and divides the land between Ziba and Mephiboshet.

How should we understand these episodes? Both Ziba and Mephiboshet cannot be telling the truth. Since there is no omniscient narrator to reveal which character is lying, the text remains ambiguous. Some commentators defend one character and some defend the other. Other commentators claim that the text purposely leaves open the question of guilt.[167] There is evidence that Mephiboshet is telling the truth. His eloquence, physical condition (e.g., the disability that pre-

---

[166] Schipper, 98-99.

[167] One scholar, for example, thinks that we are meant to be in the position of judgment just as David is (Lasine, 65). Another suggests that the fact that the narrator does not support either character is a subtle way of showing contempt for both Mephiboshet and Ziba as members of the House of Saul (Conroy, 106). Schipper has an excellent survey of various opinions on Mephiboshet and Ziba on p. 37.

vents him from traveling to meet David, the disheveled appearance that could indicate that he has been mourning for David since David fled), and concern for the king's welfare, all support Mephiboshet's claim that Ziba deceived him.[168] Ziba, on the other hand, makes the claim that his only concern is about David's welfare, and that his possession of the land is far less important than David's safety. This, if taken at face value, seems to further support Ziba's description of the events. In addition, how fitting that we question Mephiboshet's sincerity in his use of mourning rites just as we question David's intense public mourning for Saul, and his sons and supporters.[169]

Victim or Villain?

The text raises crucial questions about motivations and deception that can and should be discussed. We may also wish to know how Mephiboshet's disability affects readers. Further, are the commentators generally sympathetic toward Mephiboshet because they feel sorry for him, or because they cannot imagine a disabled person as anything more than a victim, certainly not as a political figure? Does the narrator make the text ambiguous on purpose, so as to multiply and enhance its possible meanings? Or does the narrator think the message is obvious and assume that no reader would think Mephiboshet is an acceptable heir to the throne?

Mephiboshet's disability probably has serious effects on the quality of his life. His self-image seems poor, as is evidenced by his referring to himself as a "dead dog" (2 Samuel 9:8). While this expression may simply be an ancient Near Eastern stock phrase used in conversation between a commoner and a king,[170] it is not common in the Bible.

---

[168] Fokkelman, 32.

[169] See, e.g., 2 Samuel 1:11-27; 3:31-39; 4:9-12.

[170] See, e.g., its use in the letters from both Lachish and Mari. The Lachish letters are

During his flight from Saul, David calls to Saul, and describes himself as a "dead dog" (1 Samuel 24:15), emphasizing his insignificance in comparison with the king, and indicating that there is no value in Saul's pursuit of him.[171] Mephiboshet may use the term with David to balance his obsequiousness and self-confidence and to signify that he feels degraded by his physical limitations. However, given that David does not have a shred of low self-esteem when he calls himself a "dead dog," this is not strong evidence. At the same time that David debases himself before Saul, he calls on God to judge between the two of them, a challenge he seems to expect to win. Therefore, it may be that Mephiboshet uses the term in the same savvy way as David, to defuse a delicate political situation.

Disabling Self Image

Good self-esteem is a critical concern for people with physical disabilities. Since the way a person is treated by others helps shape self-esteem, the degree to which a disabled person feels respected, provided for, and loved can determine whether he or she feels more able, or more disabled.[172] Given the frequent references in the text to Mephiboshet's handicap, his treatment, in his eyes, may underscore his disability.

In addition to the narrator's relatively frequent references to Mephiboshet's disability, Mephiboshet himself mentions his challenge

---

clay tablets written in ancient Hebrew found near the city of Lachish and were written close to the destruction of Jerusalem in 586 BCE. They are a record of the period of time right before the Babylonians conquered.The Mari letters are a large collection of tablets written in Akkadian from the city of Mari, in ancient Mesopotamia from the nineteenth century BCE.

[171] Other interesting cases include Avishai, from David's camp, who refers to someone who is bothering David as a "dead dog" (2 Samuel 16:9). Two other verses make it clear that the appellation "dog" refers to a person of comparatively low social class or standing (1 Samuel 17:43; 2 Kings 8:13).

[172] Buscaglia, 167.

and seems willing to talk about it freely. For example, when David accuses Mephiboshet of abandoning him in a time of need, Mephiboshet explains that he himself was abandoned by the servant who was supposed to help him prepare the donkey, a task Mephiboshet could not do alone (2 Samuel 19:25-29). It is not really necessary for Mephiboshet to go into such detail, particularly about his physical limitations. However, Mephiboshet is either comfortable enough with himself to talk about his legs,[173] or has so thoroughly absorbed the image others have of him that he speaks about his disability as a matter of fact.

Disabled Not Singled Out

There are two terms in the text for Mephiboshet's disability. Both the narrator and Ziba describe Mephiboshet as *"nekheh raglayim"* (2 Samuel 4:4; 9:3), a phrase that occurs in the Bible only in reference to Mephiboshet, and is best translated as "stricken in the feet."[174] Both the narrator and Mephiboshet use the term *piseach,* meaning "lame" (2 Samuel 4:4; 19:27). This term appears elsewhere in the Bible to classify groups of individuals who are lame, blind, or otherwise disadvantaged. *Piseach* is a word that does not seem derogatory in context. With it, the Bible shows that it does not view the disabled differently from people who require any kind of help. Rather, the Bible groups people with disabilities, whose needs may be lifelong, together with others who have shorter-term needs, such as the poor, widows, orphans, pregnant women, and women who have just given birth.[175] By

---

[173] This comfort in discussing disabilities instead of disguising them is generally considered helpful and healthy (Buscaglia, 174-75).

[174] Fox (1999), 167. Isaiah 66:2 mentions people who are *"nekheh ruach,"* meaning "brokenhearted," and Psalm 35:15 discusses *"nekhim,"* or "wretches." These other references support the negative connotations of the word.

[175] Some verses refer to the prohibition against bringing sacrifices that have defects,

placing all of these people in a single category, the Bible teaches that the community must offer equal support to all rather than separate out those with permanent disabilities.[176]

A difficult section of the narrative occurs when David conquers Jerusalem. When David tries to take the city for his capital, the occupying Jebusites bar his entry, saying that even the blind and the lame are capable of fighting him off. However, David conquers the city and makes it clear that the blind and the lame are not welcome, associating them with his enemies. "The king and his men went to Jerusalem, against the Jebusites who inhabited the land. It was said to David: 'You will not get in here unless you remove all the blind and the lame,' meaning that David would not be able to enter here. But David captured the Stronghold of Zion; that is, the City of David. On that day, David said: 'Whoever strikes a Jebusite, will reach the water channel, and (attack) the lame and the blind who are hated by David.' Therefore it is said: 'No one who is blind or lame will enter the House'" (2 Samuel 5:6-8).[177] These are incredibly difficult verses, and scholars offer many interpretations to try to understand their meaning. Some say that the Jebusites are boasting about their prowess when they make their claim about the disabled. Some believe that the blind and the lame actually incite the Jebusites against David. Is David's hatred for the disabled so great that he will not allow them

---

and against people with physical disabilities approaching the altar (Leviticus 21:18; Deuteronomy 15:21; Malachi 1:8,13). In other sections, God's miraculous nature is revealed either when God causes disabilities to disappear (Isaiah 35:6), or helps even people who are weak (including those with disabilities, and pregnant and new mothers) to return to Jerusalem (Jeremiah 31:7). One of Job's righteous acts is to help the needy, such as the blind or physically disabled, and the poor, widows, and orphans (Job 29:15).

[176] See the discussion on the terminology referring to Jacob's disability in the Introduction.

[177] Olyan understands that the term "the blind and the lame" in 2 Samuel 5:8 may be an inclusive term, meaning to include people with all disabilities (28-29).

into Jerusalem, or is he encouraging his forces to strike so that Jerusalem will not be filled with people who have been disabled in battle?[178] Could David be trying to establish Jerusalem as a sacred city, which, from his perspective, would exclude the disabled?[179]

David's Distaste for the Disabled

Despite the ambiguity of these verses, it is clear that before David meets Mephiboshet, the text declares unequivocally that David hates the disabled (2 Samuel 5:8). How does this statement affect an interpretation of David when he invites Mephiboshet to eat at the king's table? Is he little more than politically astute, or is he loyal and caring? Does David change his attitude toward the disabled? Is David's original position born from prejudice, so that once Mephiboshet, Jonathan's courteous, dignified, disabled son comes before him, David alters his view? Has David learned that prejudice derives from ignorance, and that once we come face to face with the person or thing we loathe, we become more accepting? Since all of these readings have merit and find support in the text, it is up to each reader to draw conclusions about David.

Questioning our Assumptions and the Assumptions of the Text

Little can be said with certainty about Mephiboshet because the

---

[178] For a fuller analysis of different points of view, see McCarter, 137-40.

[179] According to Jeremy Schipper, this verse leads us to try to come to terms with the understanding of disability in this text. He emphasizes that disability is used in this text as a method of theologizing or reflecting on Israel's history. In other words, disability is a complex motif that allows for the text to distinguish between insiders and outsiders, and to highlight Israel's possibilities and limitations. Schipper notes that the Books of Samuel and Kings do not have a single perspective on Israel, but, rather, just as the characterization of Mephiboshet is ambiguous, and just as his disability causes him to be both a royal insider, and an individual who is an outsider, so, too, the view of Israel and Israel's possibilities and limitations are multilayered and ambivalent (Schipper, 128ff.).

Bible does not say much about him. Does he support David? Is he waiting for an opportune moment to claim the throne, or is he following faithfully in his father's footsteps, acknowledging David as the rightful king? While commentators attribute many positive traits to Mephiboshet, including loyalty, purity, dignity,[180] honesty,[181] graciousness, and altruism,[182] they do not mention courage and strength. However, a close look reveals that he is a man of integrity and courage, a man who never asks for anything not offered to him. In addition, he carries on in the midst of reminders of his disability. Why then do commentators and readers often fail to recognize his inner strength?

It is time to appreciate what it must have taken for this man who could not even prepare his own means of transportation to function as a member of the court. As we analyze the Bible's attitude toward the physically disabled, we must review what the commentators say and their role in shaping how we view biblical characters with disabilities. Similarly, as we analyze Jacob and question his motivations and actions with his brother, his daughter, and his sons, we should also take into account that by the time he received his new name and sense of mission, he himself was a man who limped, a man who was permanently physically harmed by his connection with the Divine. We must also question our own assumptions about disabilities as honestly and fearlessly as we question Jacob, Ziba, David, the biblical narrator, and the commentators. Perhaps this questioning will allow us to reread the text with greater attention to—and admiration for—Mephiboshet and Jacob.

---

[180] Fokkelman, 28-40.
[181] Lasine, 65.
[182] Dalglish, 350.

Biblical personalities and depression

The language of the Bible is sparse. It expresses vast ideas with few words, often without explanatory details, digressions, or narration. This holds especially true for the inner lives of characters. While dialogue and action, as well as the voice of the narrator, occasionally open up a character's thoughts and feelings, the interpretation of characters in the Bible is usually up to the reader. A text that begs for its characters to be explained is the Akedah, or Binding of Isaac (Genesis 22), a narrative fraught with tension that is barely expressed.[183] The text does not state how Abraham, Isaac, and perhaps even Sarah must feel about the horrific ordeal. On the contrary, it is so stark that commentators, novelists, poets, and visual artists have all tried to fill the gaps.[184] Reading between the lines of the Bible makes it possible to hypothesize that several characters suffer from depression. In particular, Jonah, Hannah, and Naomi all act depressed, although in varying degrees and for differing reasons.[185] A variety of words and terms express their troubled feelings. Jonah acts angry and resentful (Jonah 4:1), and ultimately feels so deeply grieved (4:9) that he retreats into himself and thinks about suicide several times (Chs. 1, 4). Hannah feels sad (1 Samuel 1:8),[186] bitter or wretched (1:10), suffering (1:11), unhappy (1:15),[187] and full of anguish and distress (1:16). Naomi describes feeling lonely, bitter (Ruth 1:13, 20), and deserted (1:21).

---

[183] See, e.g., the classic statement of this thesis in Auerbach, "Odysseus' Scar."

[184] For a standard analysis of the technique of gap filling, see Sternberg, 186-229.

[185] Saul is another biblical character who exhibits many of the characteristics of depression. He is not included in this discussion because his case is very complex and appears to include many other psychological issues as well. An interesting analysis of Saul's emotional and mental instability can be found in Olyan, 70-71.

[186] Literally, "having a heart gone bad."

[187] Literally, "heavy of spirit."

While depression varies from individual to individual, the disorder often involves a cluster of specific physical and emotional symptoms. These include irritable, anxious, or sad moods; significant changes in appetite; a marked increase or decrease in energy; loss of interest and pleasure in routine activities; physical aches and pains; decreased sex drive; feelings of worthlessness; psychotic or delusional thinking; and thoughts of self-harm or death.[188] A depressed person often dwells on or exaggerates memories of losses or failures and feels pessimistic.[189] Feelings of worthlessness and hopelessness can overwhelm a sufferer to the point that life becomes a burden and thoughts of death predominate. An individual need not have all of these symptoms to receive a diagnosis of depression. Like many actual depression patients, Jonah, Hannah, and Naomi each have only some of the signs of the illness.

Jonah

Jonah, the reluctant prophet, is compelled by God to prophesy a warning to Nineveh, a foreign community. After God thwarts Jonah's attempts to escape this mission, Jonah ultimately delivers the divine threat to a surprisingly receptive people. Nevertheless, the Ninevites' positive and repentant response, unique in the Bible, does not alleviate Jonah's frustration and disgust. At the end of the book, Jonah grasps God's message and desires no better than he does at the beginning.

Jonah's book-long stasis contrasts starkly with the Ninevites' metamorphosis as they (and their animals) change their ways and become a righteous nation. Jonah's conduct supports reading him as a person who has lost control of his life and become depressed. In addition, his

---

[188] Papolos and Papolos, 8.
[189] Ibid., 5.

inability to grasp God's demands and desires, despite God's repeated attempts to teach him, supports the hypothesis that he is learning disabled.[190] Given that having a learning disability can often result in depression, it is plausible that Jonah could have both conditions.

Educators have recognized that depression can accompany or result from a learning disability.[191] A learning disability can affect the way a person understands, remembers, or communicates information.[192] An individual with any or all of these difficulties may have a hard time processing cues, making sense of information, or grasping large concepts. The sense that one is missing important ideas or is unable to comprehend the information swirling through one's environment can be disheartening and frustrating. For this reason, and since people with learning disabilities often struggle in a world that is either insensitive to or unaware of their difficulties, they are susceptible to depression.

That Jonah does not seem to understand God's plan or desires is evident when he feels sad that God spares the Ninevites (Jonah 4:1-4). In response to Jonah's lack of understanding, God tries to teach Jonah with a short but pointed lesson (Jonah 4:6-11). God provides Jonah with a gourd to shelter him from the blazing sun. Just as Jonah is enjoying this relief, God removes the gourd, leaving Jonah exposed. Jonah's original joy in the plant immediately turns into distress and further suicidal thinking. Although God means for the analogy to instruct Jonah that his sorrow over the gourd's demise, as great as it may be, cannot compare in magnitude to God's sorrow if God's creations (e.g., the Ninevites) are destroyed, it never is clear that Jonah comprehends.

---

[190] I thank Rabbi Neil Gillman, who first brought this idea to my attention.
[191] Smith and Strick, 77-83.
[192] Smith and Strick, 5.

Jonah's learning disability can be seen in a number of ways in which he thinks and in which he interacts with others. He misses basic concepts, such as cause and effect, and cannot connect events and ideas effectively. He reacts to each occurrence in his life as a discrete unit, rejoicing over the gourd and feeling suicidal because of the sun, rather than seeing the larger picture. In other words, he does not grasp that God is using the fate of the gourd to teach a lesson. Nor does he make the cognitive leap between God's analogy and his own experiences.

Jonah's grasp of God's ways does not develop over the course of the book, providing further evidence of his learning disability. In Chapter 4, after Nineveh is spared, Jonah expresses his displeasure at the turn of events: "O Lord! Isn't this just what I said when I was still in my own country? That is why I fled beforehand to Tarshish. For I know that You are a compassionate and gracious God, slow to anger, abounding in kindness, renouncing punishment. Please, Lord, take my life, for I would rather die than live" (Jonah 4:2-3). He claims that Nineveh's happy ending justifies his flight from Tarshish. That is, all the subsequent major events, from the storm at sea to his ingestion by the fish, each of which Jonah could have interpreted as a life-altering miracle, have no impact on his understanding of how God works in the world. Jonah's failure to advance his thinking fits with the hypothesis that he is learning disabled. Although God tries to teach him through different modalities, including direct speech and various forms of drama, Jonah does not learn the lesson.

In contrast to this reading, it is also possible to claim that Jonah stubbornly believes in strict justice and does not leave room for compassion and rehabilitation. According to this view, it is not that Jonah does not learn from God or understand God's teaching, but rather, that Jonah does not agree with God and does his best to resist and maintain his own, rigid beliefs. Often, it is hard to differentiate between an individual's tenacious adherence to a belief and his or her lack of understanding due to a learning disability. This can lead to a missed diagnosis and unwarranted accusations that an individual lacks empathy or is unwilling to consider the opinions of others.

Jonah's sad plight reflects real life. "Young people with learning disabilities often are accused of stubbornness, insensitivity, laziness, irresponsibility, carelessness, and lack of cooperation. Sometimes their low achievement is blamed on indifference to their parents' and their teachers' wishes and unwillingness to apply themselves."[193] Perhaps those who have accused Jonah of being stubborn, disobedient, and insensitive have misplaced their condemnation. They blame Jonah instead of sensitively understanding his disability.

Form and content often parallel each other in narrative texts of the Bible. In other words, the structure of the text can echo what the words express. This phenomenon is evident in Jonah, as the repetitive structure of the book as a whole parallels the lack of development in Jonah's thought process. Specifically, the first pair of chapters parallels the second pair in structure, content, style, and form.[194] Even a cursory reading of the first two verses of the first and third chapters alerts us that there is significant repetition (see, e.g., Jonah 1:1-3 and 3:1-3). This symmetry of form and content, which mirrors Jonah's lack of cognitive progress and learning, justifies reading Jonah as learning disabled. In keeping with this theory, it is relevant that the Book of Jonah concludes with an unanswered question. The hanging question highlights both God's frustration at failing to teach Jonah and Jonah's inability to truly answer God's question. Sadly, in both cases there is

---

[193] Smith and Strick, 82.
[194] This structure has been beautifully laid out and explicated by Phyllis Trible in *Rhetorical Criticism*, 109-225.

no sense of closure.

Generalized lethargy and apathy are common symptoms of depression. Jonah exhibits these behaviors as he reacts to God's commands and warnings. Jonah is the only prophet who actually runs away from God and tries to escape by sea (Jonah 1:3ff). In fact, while God commands Jonah to "get up and go" to Nineveh, Jonah "goes down" instead. Repetition of the word for "to go down"[195] highlights Jonah's outer behavior and inner mood. On the ship, Jonah repeats his avoidance behavior and then becomes lethargic. During the commotion and panic of the storm, when the sailors cry out to their gods, Jonah descends to the bottom of the boat and falls asleep (Jonah 1:5). Given the noise from the storm and the crew, as well as the shaking of the boat, it is remarkable that Jonah can sleep. It is equally astonishing that Jonah retreats from the scene during a dramatic crisis.

A number of contrasts between the conduct of the sailors and Jonah further support the hypothesis that he is depressed. While the seamen immediately react to the disaster, Jonah initially goes to sleep and responds later. Whereas their inner terror transforms into active, outward, panicked behavior, Jonah's actions of descending below deck and falling asleep lead him to become completely passive. Further, his withdrawal is out of sync with the ship, to which the text ascribes thoughts: "the ship thought it would break up" (Jonah 1:4).[196] The ship seems more responsive to the catastrophe than Jonah. Jonah's unusual, passive reaction to the terrifying and life-threatening storm may reflect a depression-caused lethargy. Like Hannah and Naomi, Jonah is silent when a well person would respond. When the ship's captain cries out to Jonah that he should not be sleeping during the

---

[195] The root *yrd* repeats three times, with a fourth time contained in another word as a pun, *vayeradem*, "he fell asleep." Greenstein, "The Old Testament as Literature," 569; see also Trible, *Rhetorical Criticism*, 134-35.

[196] Trible, *Rhetorical Criticism*, 135.

storm, Jonah does not answer (Jonah 1:6). This is Jonah's usual man-ner. Just as he does not respond to God, he remains silent until the sailors directly confront him.

Jonah shows he realizes he is in grave trouble when he tells the sailors that he ran away from God. When he orders the sailors to throw him overboard to quiet the storm, Jonah seems to want to die, and perhaps exhibits suicidal tendencies (Jonah 1:10-12). He does not consider any other ways to save the ship, the sailors, and himself. While the sailors call to their gods for help, Jonah never addresses God even though God spoke to him earlier. Unlike Jonah, the sailors are so committed to Jonah's life that they put themselves in jeop-ardy by trying to row to shore before agreeing to his demand (Jonah 1:13).

The sailors are distraught about the prospect of tossing Jonah into the water, believing that it is an act of murder (Jonah 1:14). As we have seen, even strangers seem to care about Jonah's life more than he does: "From a psychological vantage point Jonah behaves like an acutely depressed person—hopeless, helpless, and feeling as if he were carrying a contagious disease. His injunction to the sailors to dispose of him is a gesture of suicide."[197] Depression can deaden the sufferer's imagination and hopes about the future. He or she can feel isolated and disconnected from other people and from the current of life, past, present, and future. Throughout the first chapter, Jonah undergoes a steady emotional decline that culminates in suicidal thinking. The chain of events that begins when he leaves Tarshish develops from a flight from pressure into a request for help in killing himself.

After the sailors concede and throw Jonah into the water, a huge fish swallows him alive. From within its belly he says a heartfelt and

---

[197] LaCoque and LaCoque, 88.

beautiful prayer to God. He describes feeling on the edge. He has brushed close to death, but has been delivered (Jonah 2:1-10). At this point in the narrative, Jonah seems to have improved his understanding of God's desires and developed a personal stake in God's mission. This may be why Jonah pulls himself together and, in the next scene, delivers God's message to Nineveh (Jonah 3:1ff). The Ninevites react to their sentence with horror and complete contrition. As a result, God rescinds the threat and spares them.

In the final chapter, Jonah reverts to his original emotional state. He is extremely upset and resentful that God does not destroy the Ninevites. This time he speaks aloud his wish to die: "Please, Lord, take my life, for I would rather die than live" (Jonah 4:3). Just as Jonah is out of touch with the sailors and the ship near the beginning of the narrative, Jonah is out of step with the Ninevites and with God toward the end. While the Ninevites feel grateful for God' mercy, Jonah is deeply grieved by the turn of events. While the Ninevites do everything possible to preserve their lives, Jonah begs to die.[198]

Jonah understands that God is in charge. He feels totally helpless before God, Who seems like an insurmountable obstacle.[199] Jonah learns that God controls his life and that he cannot escape God's will. Both of his attempts to flee, once on a boat, and once through suicide, end in failure. In the fish, he recognizes that he has no power over his own life and that he will eventually end up following God's orders. This is why he does God's bidding as quickly as possible. Jonah's perception may explain why he reacts to the events with thoughts of suicide. In Jonah's mind, death is the only route of escape from God's control.

Jonah is exhibiting signs of "learned helplessness," a phenomenon in

---

[198] Ibid., 75.
[199] Ibid., 142.

which a person experiences that his or her responses to events do not lead to results and so the responses abate or are eliminated. Learned helplessness like Jonah's can be directly related to depression.[200] People who feel that they have no control over events in their lives are more prone to depression.[201] It is a painful paradox of depression that the feeling that events are out of control can lead to depression, and depression can lead to the feeling that events are out of control. This is Jonah's experience. His learned helplessness may actually exacerbate the depression that plagues him in Chapter 1. Many prophets reach the same point, the moment when they recognize that God controls all aspects of their lives. For example, Jeremiah cries out to God that he does not want to prophesy, but the words burn within him until they leave his mouth (Jeremiah 20:9). What distinguishes Jonah from other prophets is that he responds by withdrawing and attempting suicide. He does not follow the standard prophetic route of addressing God and interceding either for the people or for himself.[202]

Jonah makes clear how depression and learning disabilities can taint a person's grasp of the world and his or her place in it. His story also shows how easy it is to misunderstand and misjudge people with depression and learning disabilities. The tragedy of Jonah lasts well beyond the four short chapters of his story. Just as Jonah is misunderstood in the narrative about him, and just as he has been misunderstood through the ages, the depressed and the learning disabled are still misunderstood today. Ironically, there are commentators who consider Jonah the most successful prophet in the Bible, for he is the only one who brings about complete change and repentance in his

---

[200] Miller, Rosellini, and Seligman, 181-219; Abramson, Seligman, and Teasdale, 259-301.

[201] Abramson, Seligman, and Teasdale, 296.

[202] For an excellent analysis of prophetic intercession, see Yochanan Muffs, *Love and Joy*, 9-48.

charges. Unfortunately, because of his twin challenges, depression and a learning disability, he most likely believes that he is a great failure.

Hannah and Naomi

It is valuable to look at Jonah's depression in the context of other biblical characters who have their own reasons for being depressed. Hannah, Samuel's mother, is an inspiring character who lives with the heartbreak of infertility. Prior to Samuel's birth, Hannah spends many years in despair because her co-wife Peninah is fertile. Hannah's childlessness makes her insecure about her position in and value to the family, question Elkanah's devotion and love, and fear for her livelihood after he dies. Peninah's taunts and insensitive remarks worsen Hannah's worries. Hannah's trying circumstances continue for a long time: "This happened year after year: Every time she went up to the House of the Lord, the other would taunt her, so that she wept and would not eat" (1 Samuel 1:7). Her depression is not the result of one event, but rather, of a long series of upsetting experiences. As opposed to Jonah, however, her depression is the result of a specific element in her life, her infertility, that, when changed, allows her to quickly heal. Jonah's depression, sadly, is based on a permanent individual characteristic, his learning disability, which makes it that much harder to recover.

Hannah is also blessed to be supported by a husband who makes a real effort to encourage her. Hannah's gloom is obvious to her husband Elkanah, who asks, "Hannah, why are you crying and why aren't you eating? Why are you so sad? Am I not more devoted to you than ten sons?" (1 Samuel 1:8). Elkanah does not know the cause of Hannah's sadness or how to cure it. Elkanah, like the family members of many depressed individuals, has no idea how to lift the mood of his loved one. As a first response to depression in a relative, families tend to offer attention, reassurance, and assistance with routine tasks. However, the loved one often cannot or does not accept help.[203] This occurs with Hannah. Although Elkanah shows his concern, she does not respond to him. Jonah, on the other hand, seems to face his difficulties alone, without partners on his journey.

Depression, such as in the case of Jonah, can lead an individual to feel so hopeless and devastated that he or she is inert and unable to change the situation.[204] Thus, it is remarkable that Hannah even thinks to visit the temple to pray and make a vow to God. In all of the narratives of barren and fertile co-wives in the Bible, Hannah is the only woman who uses a personal relationship with God to solve her problem.

In the beginning of the narrative, Hannah is a woman with a good reason to feel depressed, a woman whose sadness shows in the way she looks and acts. Hannah's ability to take charge of her challenge, particularly when she is depressed, is unusual and notable. She seeks out a source of comfort, shares her immense burden, and sets herself on the path to recovery. The comparison between Jonah and Hannah is instructive. Hannah's depression is more concentrated on one issue. She lives within a family unit and a community that, while trying, also provides support. Seeing Hannah's struggles throws Jonah's difficulties into extra relief and underscores the lifelong situation he faced alone. It is therefore not surprising that he does not recover the way Hannah does. Still, we would be remiss if we did not allow Hannah to inspire us with how she heals herself.

Another interesting comparison is with Naomi in the Book of

---

[203] Papolos and Papolos, 267.
[204] Perry, 10-11.

Ruth. The book begins with the destruction of a family. After Naomi and her family migrate from Judah to Moab to escape a famine, her husband and two sons die, leaving her without blood relatives and feeling responsible for her foreign daughters-in-law, Orpah and Ruth (Ruth 1:1-5). When Naomi decides to journey back to Judah, the young women try to join her. Naomi manages to convince Orpah to return to Moab. However, Ruth travels on with her mother-in-law. She declares loyalty to Naomi, her people, and her God (Ruth 1:16-17). Naomi tries to discourage both women from joining her by painting a very bleak picture of her life. She anticipates a dark future, without family and oppressed by God: "My lot is far more bitter than yours, for the hand of the Lord has struck out against me" (Ruth 1:13). Ultimately, she simply ignores Ruth's offers of assistance,[205] and, with heartbreaking words, Naomi says that God has singled her out for ill treatment (Ruth 1:20-21). Classic symptoms of depression include thoughts and feelings of worthlessness, sometimes in combination with excessive guilt that may become grossly unreasonable or delusional.[206] Naomi's harsh self-perception and sense that God is against

---

[205] While it is startling that Naomi does not answer Ruth's lyrical statement of devotion, it is possible to understand Naomi's ungrateful silence as a symptom of deep depression. A characteristic of the disorder is a diminishing or deadening of the tone, speed, or quantity of speech. A woman who suffered from depression wrote words that Naomi might have used to describe herself:

"During depression the world disappears. Language itself. One has nothing to say. Nothing. No small talk, no anecdotes. Nothing can be risked on the board of talk. Because the inner voice is so urgent in its own discourse: How shall I live? How shall I manage in the future? Why should I go on? There is nothing ahead, my powers are failing, I am aging. I do not want to continue into the future as I see it... And so, on the little surface of life, these deeper questions being so peremptory, there is nothing to advance by way of conversation. One's real state of mind is a source of shame. So one is necessarily silent about it, leaving nothing else for subject matter. Therefore, one listens, bullied by others' talk, that very talk an invasion."

Kate Millet, in *The Loony Bin Trip* as quoted in Papolos and Papolos, 15.
[206] Papolos and Papolos, 8.

her may signal a deep clinical depression brought on by the death of her husband and two sons in a foreign land. Like Jonah, Naomi sees no future for herself, but she has the advantage of facing this struggle in the context of family and community, a great blessing indeed.

Naomi first begins to have hope for the future when she hears of Ruth's meeting with Boaz. She starts to respond as if awakening from sleep. Prior to the meeting, when Ruth first suggests going out to glean, Naomi simply tells her to do so (Ruth 2:2) without thought of the potential harvest or the dangers that might lurk in the fields. Following the encounter with Boaz, Naomi acknowledges the risks and suggests how Ruth can protect herself from predatory men (Ruth 2:22). At last, Naomi seems to notice the people and things around her, to come back to life. Jonah who sees God's miraculous work around him in overt ways is not able to bring himself out of the depression in which he has sunk. Naomi, on the other hand, through the help of family and community, is able to find recovery and help in just the hint of the Divine through a new understanding of "coincidence."

Conclusion

Each of the characters that we have examined in this chapter teaches something unique about depression. Jonah never seems to recover from his depressed state. He is as sad and confused at the end of the book as he is in the beginning. Jonah's suicidal thoughts appear in Chapters 1 and 4, forming a frame within which he is too gloomy to grow. On the other hand, both Hannah and Naomi recover from their depressions through the help of understanding their relationships to God and to their families and communities.

God's role in these narratives is as varied as the characters' depression. For Hannah, God is an approachable presence, a target for her plea. God does not initiate the conversation with Hannah but responds when sought (1 Samuel 1:19). God's help to Naomi comes in a slightly different form, through happenstance, such as Ruth's happening to glean in Boaz's field so that she is in a position to come to his attention (Ruth 2:3-4). It is commonly agreed that coincidence in the Bible signals God's actions and presence. (As one commentator eloquently put it, "Chance, that code for the Divine." [207]) Ultimately, it is Naomi's understanding of the coincidences in her life that allow her to see God's activity and assistance. This understanding, combined with Ruth's continuing aid and support lead Naomi to begin a recovery. With Jonah, God *is* more hands-on, actively working miracles and speaking to him to explain the meaning of divine actions. However, for Jonah even this is not enough, and he remains in the dark.

Looking at these three texts together leads to some important conclusions. That God takes a different approach to each character is highly significant. God tailors divine intervention and activity to individual needs, being available when Hannah asks, working through the people around Naomi, and overtly teaching Jonah. God's sensitivity to individual differences reminds us to respect individual needs and styles. God's responses to Hannah, Naomi, and Jonah also make a statement about God's sense of the importance of emotional well being. God seems to understand the extent to which emotional devastation affects each character and tries to help each one overcome it. As depression has become widespread among schoolchildren, we should make every effort to follow God's lead in recognizing the dangers of the disorder and in doing all we can to tailor a response to reach each person who suffers from it.

---

[207] Trible, *Rhetoric of Sexuality*, 178.

Conclusion

We have seen through our study that the biblical text acknowledges that disabilities exist. Further, our tradition calls upon us to understand that all people, at every level of ability, deserve understanding and compassion. How marvelous it is to see this ancient text's sensitivity in its approach to disability! The full picture is seen when we combine biblical legal and narrative literature. Blindness is a case in point. The Bible explicitly demands compassion for the blind: "You are not to insult the deaf; before the blind you are not to place a stumbling-block: rather, you are to hold your God in awe; I am YHWH!" (Leviticus 19:14). This famous, beautiful verse unambiguously states that consideration toward people with disabilities is an important element of a God-fearing life of holiness.

Although the verse gives the general rule, it does not say anything about the abilities, thoughts, concerns, or challenges of the individual blind or deaf person.[208] It is up to the narrative texts of the Bible to provide examples of individuals whose struggles with disabilities give context to these rules.

Two of the patriarchs in Genesis become blind in old age. Both Isaac and Jacob are put in the position of blessing their descendants while unable to see them (Genesis 27 and 48). Sightlessness is central to both narratives. The account of Jacob conferring blessing on Joseph's children offers a great lesson. At the moment that Jacob is poised to bless his grandsons, Joseph positions the children so that Jacob's right hand will rest on Manasseh, Joseph's firstborn. In re-

---

[208] Unfortunately, there are no biblical narrative texts that give us true insight into the life of the hearing impaired. This may be because in ancient times it was harder to integrate deaf individuals who could not speak into the life of the community.

sponse, "blind" Jacob crosses his hands so that his right hand touches Ephraim, the younger brother. When Joseph objects that his father has erred, Jacob asserts that the switch was deliberate. Although Joseph fears that his father is confused because of blindness, it is in fact Jacob who sees what must be done. Joseph assumes that his father's blindness indicates a mental deficit or lack of comprehension. In reality, Jacob's actions highlight his clear thinking and prove that it is Joseph who has difficulty seeing to the heart of the matter. Lack of sight does not mean lack of insight. Blindness, a physical disability, is no indication of mental or spiritual weakness. Thus, the commandment to protect the blind is not motivated by pity for the disabled, and is not meant to imply that the blind person is a burden to society. Rather, it prescribes the kindness we are expected show to those who need extra consideration.

Writing this book has renewed my awe for the Bible's layering and artistry. I am grateful for the complexity and the ambiguity of the text that allow me the opportunity to find within its pages the here-and-now relevance of characters with special needs. I am struck anew in contemplating the Bible's contemporary attitude and applications and feel privileged to be able to spend my life, both religiously and academically, in conversation with it. To the extent that the Bible is a repository of Israel's historic encounter with God, this study shows that one of God's treasured roles is Master Teacher of special needs students. God adapts the divine plan to suit Isaac's intellectual limitations by minimizing Isaac's covenantal obligations. God permits Joseph, one of the Divine Instructor's most gifted students, to learn inductively, thereby allowing him to actively participate in the process as revelation unfolds. God mentors Moses throughout his life, prodding him to grapple with his disability. Even Esau, surely one of

God's most challenging students, though victimized by generations of exegetes, is never abandoned by his Teacher. Although learning is painful for Esau, God guides him toward an appropriate lifestyle. And Esau is blessed, by his father and by God. In his life, Esau enjoys more happiness, camaraderie, and inner peace than his more "fortunate" brother, Jacob, ever knows.

Perhaps, however, we can take the role of God in this endeavor one step further. I conclude this book with a personal note. I have lived a fair amount of my life with a physical disability, and at various times have needed to come to terms with using a cane. At one point in that struggle, I came to focus on a biblical verse which is familiar, but which I suddenly read in a new light. Psalm 23:4 states that God's "rod and staff comfort" us, which is generally understood in the context of God as shepherd, leading the flock with a staff. At that moment, however, I focused on the word *mish'antekha*, which, though generally translated as "staff," literally means, "that which you lean upon." Might we understand from this verse that God sometimes needs to lean on a stick? Could the Psalmist be telling us that God uses a cane? "Your rod and Your staff"—that is, the image of a God compelled to take recourse to a source of support—"comforts me," and may offer a refreshing perspective to all who contend with disabilities. It provides an image of God that is resonant for those of us subject to personal limitations and challenges. And who amongst us is not beset with challenges? There are many more doors ahead of us to open in approaching the biblical text from the perspective of disability studies that can lead to spiritual and emotional growth.

In the statement that provides the frontispiece to this study, Helen Keller observes: "I thank God for my handicaps for through them I have found myself, my work, and my God." As readers of the Bible, we all have a great deal to learn from disabilities... and from those whose lives are most intimately touched by them.

Bibliography

Abrams, Judith Z. *Judaism and Disability*. Washington, D.C.: Gallaudet University Press, 1998.

—. "*Metsora(at) KaShaleg*: Leprosy and Challenges to Authority in the Tanach." *Jewish Bible Quarterly* 21 (1993): 41-45.

—. "Was Isaac Disabled?" *Reconstructionist* 56.1 (1990): 20-21.

Abramson, Lyn Y., Martin E. P. Seligman, and John D. Teasdale. "Learned Helplessness in Humans: Critique and Reformulation." *Essential Papers on Depression*. Ed. James C. Coyne. New York: New York University Press, 1985. 259-301.

Ages, Arnold. "Dreamer, Schemer, Slave and Prince." *Bible Review* 14 (1998): 47-52.

Alper, Sandra, Patrick J. Schloss, and Cynthia N. Schloss. *Families of Students with Disabilities*. Boston: Allyn and Bacon, 1994.

Alter, Robert. *The Art of Biblical Narrative*. New York: Basic, 1981.

—, *Genesis*. New York: Norton, 1996.

Amit, Yairah. "'Manoah Promptly Followed His Wife' (Judges 13:11): On the Place of the Woman in Birth Narratives." *A Feminist Companion to Judges*. Ed. Athalya Brenner. Sheffield, Eng.: Sheffield Academic Press, 1993. 146-56.

Arllen, Nancy L., Robert A. Gable, and Jo M. Hendrickson. "Toward an Understanding of the Origins of Aggression." *Preventing School Failure* 38.3 (1994): 18-23.

Attridge, Harold, et al. *Discoveries in the Judaean Desert XIII: Qumran Cave 4*. Vol. 8. Oxford: Clarendon Press, 1994.

Auerbach, Erich, "Odysseus' Scar," *Mimesis*. Princeton: Princeton University Press, 1953.

Baroff, George S. *Mental Retardation: Nature, Cause, and Management*. Washington, D.C.: Hemisphere, 1986.

Berkowitz, Mozelle, Harriet Cook, and Mary Jo Haughey. "A Non-Traditional Fluency Program Developed for the Public School Setting." *Language, Speech, and Hearing Services in Schools* 25 (1994): 94-99.

Berlin, Adele. *Poetics and Interpretation of Biblical Narrative.* Sheffield, Eng.: Almond, 1983.

Birch, Bruce, "Impairment as a Condition in Biblical Scholarship." *This Abled Body: Rethinking Disabilities in Biblical Studies,* Ed. Hector Avalos, Sarah J. Melcher, and Jeremy Schipper. Atlanta: Society of Biblical Literature Semeia Studies, 2007. 185-196.

Blake, James Neal. *Speech, Language, and Learning Disorders: Education and Therapy.* Springfield, IL: Thomas, 1971.

Bleich, J. David. "Torah Education of the Mentally Retarded." *Journal of Halacha and Contemporary Society* 4 (1982): 79-92.

Blood, Gordon W. "A Behavioral-Cognitive Therapy Program for Adults who Stutter: Computers and Counseling." *Journal of Communication Disorders* 28 (1995): 165-80.

Bogdan, Robert and Steven J. Taylor. *The Social Meaning of Mental Retardation.* New York: Teachers College Press, 1994.

Boyles, Nancy S. and Darlene Contadino. *Parenting a Child with Attention Deficit/Hyperactivity Disorder.* Los Angeles: Lowell, 1996.

Buscaglia, Leo. *The Disabled and Their Parents.* New York: Holt, 1983.

Chamrad, Diana L., Nancy M. Robinson, and Paul M. Janos. "Consequences of Having a Gifted Sibling: Myths and Realities." *Gifted Child Quarterly* 39 (1995): 135-45.

Clarizio, Harvey F. "Conduct Disorder: Developmental Considerations." *Psychology in the Schools* 34 (1997): 253-65.

Clark, Barbara. *Growing Up Gifted.* Columbus: Merrill, 1983.

Colangelo, Nicholas and Penny Brower. "Gifted Youngsters and Their Siblings: Long-Term Impact of Labeling on Their Academic and Personal Self-Concepts." *Roeper Review* 10 (1987): 101-3.

Conroy, Charles. *Absalom Absalom!: Narrative and Language in 2 Samuel 13-20.* Rome: Biblical Institute, 1978.

Cooper, Eugene B. and Crystal S. Cooper. "Treating Fluency Disordered Adolescents." *Journal of Communication Disorders* 28 (1995): 125-42.

Dalglish, E. R. "Mephiboshet," *The Interpreter's Dictionary of the Bible.* Ed. George Arthur Buttrick. Vol. 3. Nashville: Abingdon, 1962.

Damrosch, David. *The Narrative Covenant: Transformations of Genre in the Growth of Biblical Literature.* San Francisco: Harper and Row, 1987.

Dickstein, Joel C. "Jewish Special Education and the Quiet Revolution." Diss. Teachers College, Columbia U, 1995.

Ehrlich, Virginia Z. *Gifted Children: A Guide for Parents and Teachers*. Englewood Cliffs, NJ: Prentice, 1982.

Elshout, Elly, et al. "Roundtable Discussion: Women with Disabilities—A Challenge to Feminist Theology." *Journal of Feminist Studies in Religion* 10 (1994): 99-134.

Exum, J. Cheryl. *Fragmented Women: Feminist (Sub)Versions of Biblical Narratives*. Pennsylvania: Trinity, 1993.

—. "Second Thoughts About Secondary Characters: Women in Exodus 1:8-2:10." *A Feminist Companion to Exodus to Deuteronomy*. Ed. Athalya Brenner. Sheffield, Eng.: Sheffield Academic Press, 1994. 75-87.

Falk, Marcia. "Reflections on Hannah's Prayer." *Out of the Garden*. Eds. Christina Bachmann and Celina Spiegel. New York: Ballantine, 1994. 94-102.

Fewell, Danna Nolan and David Gunn. *Compromising Redemption*. Louisville, KY: Westminster-Knox, 1990.

Flanigan, Patrick J., George R. Baker, and Lynn G. LaFollette. *An Orientation to Mental Retardation*. Illinois: Thomas, 1970.

Forness, Steven R., et al. "Simple Versus Complex Conduct Disorders: Identification and Phenomenology." *Behavioral Disorders* 19 (1994): 306-12.

Fox, Everett. *The Five Books of Moses*. New York: Schocken, 1995.

—. *Give Us a King!: A New English Translation of the Book of Samuel*. New York: Schocken, 1999.

Freedman, David Noel, ed. *Anchor Bible Dictionary*. New York: Doubleday, 1992. S.v. "Isaac," by Robert Martin-Achard.

Fries, Kenny, ed. *Staring Back: The Disability Experience from the Inside Out*. New York: Penguin, 1997.

Gartner, Alan, Dorothy Kerzner Lipsky, and Ann P. Turnbull. *Supporting Families with a Child with a Disability: An International Outlook*. Baltimore: Brookes, 1991.

Goitein, S. D. "Women as Creators of Biblical Genres." *Prooftexts* 8 (1988): 1-33.

Graetz, Naomi. "Did Miriam Talk Too Much?" *A Feminist Companion to Exodus to Deuteronomy*. Ed. Athalya Brenner. Sheffield, Eng.: Sheffield Academic Press, 1994. 231-42.

Greenstein, Edward L. "An Equivocal Reading of the Sale of Joseph." *Literary Intepretations of Biblical Narratives*. Ed. Kenneth R. R. Gros Louis with James S. Ackerman. Vol. 2. Nashville: Abingdon, 1982. 114-25.

—. "The Old Testament as Literature." *Harper's Bible Dictionary*. Ed. Paul Achtemeier. New York: HarperCollins, 1985.

—. "The Riddle of Samson." *Prooftexts* 1 (1981): 237-60.

Gros Louis, Kenneth R. R. "Abraham: II." *Literary Intepretations of Biblical Narratives*. Ed. Kenneth R. R. Gros Louis with James S. Ackerman. Vol. 2. Nashville: Abingdon, 1982. 71-84.

Grossman, Dan and Joel Grishaver. *Bible Play: Instant Lesson*. Los Angeles: Torah Aura, 1987.

Gruber, Les. "Moses: His Speech Impediment and Behavior Therapy." *Journal of Psychology and Judaism* 10 (1986): 5-13.

Guyette, Fred. "Joseph's Emotional Development" *Jewish Bible Quarterly* 32 (2004): 181-8.

Hardman, Michael L., Clifford J. Drew, and Winston M. Egan. *Human Exceptionality: Society, School, and Family*. Boston: Allyn and Bacon, 1999.

Hartmann, Thom. *Attention Deficit Disorder: A Different Perception*. Penn Valley, CA: Underwood-Miller, 1993.

Henkin, Alan. "The Two of Them Went Together' (Genesis 22:6): Visions of Interdependence." *Judaism* 32 (1983): 452-62.

Hentrich, Thomas. "Masculinity and Disability in the Bible." *This Abled Body: Rethinking Disabilities in Biblical Studies*, Eds. Hector Avalos, Sarah J. Melcher, and Jeremy Schipper. Atlanta: Society of Biblical Literature Semeia Studies, 2007. 73-87.

Houston, Barbara. "Gender Freedom and the Subtleties of Sexist Education." *The Gender Question in Education*. Eds. Ann Diller, Barbara Houston, Kathryn Pauly Morgan, and Maryann Ayim. Boulder: Westview, 1996. 50-63.

Hyde, Margaret O., and Elizabeth Held Forsyth. *Suicide*. New York: Watts, 1991.

Janzen, J. Gerald. "Song of Moses, Song of Miriam: Who is Seconding Whom?" *A Feminist Companion to Exodus to Deuteronomy*. Ed. Athalya Brenner. Sheffield, Eng.: Sheffield Academic Press, 1994. 187-99.

Jezer, Marty. *Stuttering: A Life Bound Up in Words*. New York: Basic, 1997.

Kaiser, Ann P., and Peggy P. Hester. "Prevention of Conduct Disorder Through

Early Intervention: A Social-Communicative Perspective." *Behavioral Disorders* 22 (1997): 117-30.

Kaminetzky, Edward. "Incorporating the Special Education Philosophy Within American Jewish Education." Diss. Teachers College, Columbia U., 1976.

Kaminsky, Joel S. "Humor and the Theology of Hope: Isaac as a Humorous Figure." *Interpretation* 54 (2000): 363-75.

Kamps, Debra M., and Melody Tankersley. "Prevention of Behavioral and Conduct Disorders: Trends and Research Issues." *Behavioral Disorders* 22 (1996): 41-8.

Keirouz, Kathryn S. "Concerns of Parents of Gifted Children: A Research Review." *Gifted Child Quarterly* 34 (1990): 56-63.

Kimchi, Rabbi David. *Sefer Hashorashim.*

Kirsch, Jonathan. *Moses: A Life.* New York: Ballantine, 1998.

Krementz, Jill. *How it Feels to Live with a Physical Disability.* New York: Simon and Schuster, 1992.

Kunin, Seth Daniel. *The Logic of Incest: A Structuralist Analysis of Hebrew Mythology.* Sheffield, Eng.: Sheffield Academic Press, 1995.

LaCocque, Andrè, and Pierre-Emmanuel LaCocque. *Jonah: A Psycho-Religious Approach to the Prophet.* Columbia, South Carolina: University of South Carolina Press, 1990.

Lanzkowsky, Shelly. "An Ancient Case of Attention Deficit Disorder." *Pediatrics* March (2006): 721.

Lasine, Stuart. "Judicial Narratives and the Ethics of Reading: The Reader as Judge of the Dispute Between Mephibosheth and Ziba." *Hebrew Studies* 30 (1989): 49-69.

Leicester, Mal, and Tessa Lovell. "Disability Voice: Educational Experience and Disability." *Disability and Society* 12 (1997): 111-18.

Lobato, Debra J. *Brothers, Sisters, and Special Needs.* Baltimore: Brookes, 1990.

Lyon, Harold C. "Realising our Potential." *Gifted Children: Looking to Their Future.* Eds. Joy Gibson and Prue Chennells. London: Latimer, 1976. 20-34.

Malul, Meir. "More on Pahad Yishaq (Genesis XXXI 42, 53) and the Oath by the 'Thigh'." *Vetus Testamentum* 35 (1985): 192-200.

Marcus, David. *From Balaam to Jonah: Anti-prophetic Satire in the Hebrew Bible.* Atlanta: Scholars Press, 1995.

Martin-Achard, Robert. "Isaac." *Anchor Bible Dictionary.* Ed. David Noel

Freedman. Vol. 3. New York: Doubleday, 1992.

Matthys, Walter. "Residential Behavior Therapy for Children with Conduct Disorders." *Behavior Modification* 21 (1997): 512-32.

McCarter, P. Kyle, Jr. *The Anchor Bible: II Samuel.* New York: Doubleday, 1984.

Melamed-Cohen, Rahamim. *The Exceptional Child and Special Education According to Jewish Sources.* Jerusalem: Sedar Ot Sasson, 1997.

Meyer, Donald J., and Patricia F. Vadasy. *Sibshops: Workshops for Siblings of Children With Special Needs.* Baltimore: Brookes, 1994.

Milgrom, Jacob. *The JPS Torah Commentary: Numbers.* Eds. Nahum Sarna and Chaim Potok. Philadelphia: Jewish Publication Society, 1990.

Miller, William R., Robert A. Rosellini, and Martin E. P. Seligman. "Learned Helplessness and Depression." *Essential Papers on Depression.* Ed. James C. Coyne. New York: New York University Press, 1985. 181-219.

Mobley, Gregory. "The Wild Man in the Bible and the Ancient Near East." *Journal of Biblical Literature* 116 (1997): 217-33.

Muffs, Yochanan. *Love and Joy: Law, Language and Religion in Ancient Israel.* New York: The Jewish Theological Seminary of America, 1992.

Napier, Augustus Y., and Carl Whitaker. *The Family Crucible: The Intense Experience of Family Therapy.* New York: HarperCollins, 1978.

Neusner, Jacob. *The Judaism Behind the Texts: The Generative Premises of Rabbinic Literature.* Vol. 3. Atlanta: Scholars Press, 1994.

Newcomer, Phyllis L., Edna Barenbaum, and Nils Pearson. "Depression and Anxiety in Children and Adolescents with Learning Disabilities, Conduct Disorders, and No Disabilities." *Journal of Emotional and Behavioral Disorders* 3 (1995): 27-39.

O'Brien, Mark. "The Contribution of Judah's Speech, Genesis 44:18-34, to the Characterization of Joseph." *The Catholic Biblical Quarterly* 59 (1997): 429-47.

Olyan, Saul M. *Disability in the Hebrew Bible: Interpreting Mental and Physical Differences.* Cambridge: Cambridge University Press, 2008.

Orenstein, Peggy. *Schoolgirls: Young Women, Self-Esteem, and the Confidence Gap.* New York: Anchor-Doubleday, 1994.

Ozick, Cynthia. "Hannah and Elkanah: Torah as the Matrix for Feminism." *Out of the Garden.* Eds. Christina Bachmann and Celina Spiegel. New York:

Ballantine, 1994. 88-93.

Papolos, Demitri, and Janice Papolos. *Overcoming Depression.* New York: Harper Perennial, 1997.

Parkyn, G. W. "Identification and Evaluation of Gifted Children." *Gifted Children: Looking to Their Future.* Eds. Joy Gibson and Prue Chennells. London: Latimer, 1976. 35-56.

Perdue, Leo G. "'Is There Anyone Left of the House of Saul...?' Ambiguity and the Characterization of David in the Succession Narrative." *Journal for the Study of the Old Testament* 30 (1984): 67-84.

Perkins, William H. *Human Perspectives in Speech and Language Disorders.* St. Louis: Mosby, 1978.

Perry, Angela R., ed. *Essential Guide to Depression* (American Medical Association). New York: Pocket Books, 1998.

Plaut, W. G. "The Strange Blessing: A Modern Midrash on Genesis 27." *Journal of the Central Conference of American Rabbis* 8 (1960): 30-4.

Pollack, Stuart. "The Speech Defect of Moses." *Jewish Bible Quarterly* 26 (1998): 121-23.

Porterfield, Kay Marie. *Straight Talk About Learning Disabilities.* New York: Facts on File, 1999.

Powell, Thomas H., and Peggy Ahrenhold Ogle. *Brothers and Sisters—A Special Part of Exceptional Families.* Baltimore: Brookes, 1985.

Prouser, Ora Horn. "The Truth About Women and Lying." *Journal for the Study of the Old Testament* 61 (1994): 15-28.

—. "The Hebrew Bible." *From Mesopotamia to Modernity*, eds. Burton L. Visotzky and David E. Fishman. Colorado: Westview Press, 1999. 9-36.

Ramig, Peter R. "Working With 7- to 12-Year-Old Children Who Stutter: Ideas for Intervention in the Public Schools." *Language, Speech, and Hearing Services in Schools* 26 (1995): 138-50.

Randall, Julia Davenport. *Blessing Esau: Experiments in High School English-teaching.* Boston: R. G. Badger, The Gorham Press, 1919.

Raphael, Rebecca. Biblical Corpora: *Representations of Disability in Hebrew Biblical Literature.* New York: T. and T. Clark, 2008.

Robbins, Paul R. *Understanding Depression.* Jefferson, NC: McFarland, 1993.

Royse, David, and Tom Edwards. "Communicating About Disability: Attitudes and Preferences of Persons with Physical Handicaps." *Rehabilitation*

Counseling Bulletin 32 (March 1989): 203-209.

Sabatino, David A. "Replacing Anger with Trust." *Reclaiming Children and Youth* 6 (1997): 167-70.

Sadker, Myra and David Sadker. *Failing at Fairness: How America's Schools Cheat Girls.* New York: Scribner's, 1994.

Sarna, Nahum. *The JPS Torah Commentary: Genesis.* Eds. Nahum Sarna and Chaim Potok. Philadelphia: Jewish Publication Society, 1989.

Savran, George W. *Telling and Retelling: Quotation in Biblical Narrative.* Bloomington, IN: Indiana University Press, 1988.

Schipper, Jeremy. *Disability Studies and the Hebrew Bible: Figuring Mephibosheth in the David Story.* New York: T. and T. Clark, 2006.

Schwartz, Yoel. *Special Child–Special Parent: The Special Child in Jewish Sources.* New York: Feldheim, 1998.

Selikowitz, Mark. *All About A.D.D.* New York: Oxford University Press, 1997.

Smith, Corinne and Lisa Strick. *Learning Disabilities: A to Z.* New York: Free, 1997.

Sommers-Flanagan, John and Rita Sommers-Flanagan. "Assessment and Diagnosis of Conduct Disorder." *Journal of Counseling and Development* 76 (1998): 189-97.

Spero, Shubert. "Jacob and Esau: The Relationship Reconsidered." *Jewish Bible Quarterly* 32 (2004): 245-50.

Spiegel, Shalom. *The Last Trial.* New York: Schocken, 1967.

Sternberg, Meir. *The Poetics of Biblical Narrative.* Bloomington, IN: Indiana University Press, 1985.

Subotnik, Rena, et al. *Genius Revisited: High IQ Children Grown Up.* Norwood, NJ: Ablex, 1993.

Thomas, Marlin. "Albert Einstein and LD: An Evaluation of the Evidence." *Journal of Learning Disabilities* 33 (2000): 149-57.

Thomson, Rosemarie Garland. "Integrating Disability Studies into the Existing Curriculum." *The Disability Studies Reader.* Ed. Lennard J. Davis. New York: Routledge, 1997. 295-306.

Thorne, Barrie. *Gender Play: Girls and Boys in School.* Piscataway, NJ: Rutgers University Press, 1993.

Trible, Phyllis. "Bringing Miriam Out of the Shadows." *A Feminist Companion to Exodus to Deuteronomy.* Ed. Athalya Brenner. Sheffield, Eng.: Sheffield

Academic Press, 1994. 166-86.

—. "Genesis 22: The Sacrifice of Sarah," in *"Not in Heaven" Coherence and Complexity in Biblical Narrative.* Eds. Jason P. Rosenblatt and Joseph C. Sitterson, Jr. Bloomington, IN: Indiana University Press, 1991. 170-91.

—. *God and the Rhetoric of Sexuality.* Philadelphia: Fortress, 1978.

—. *Rhetorical Criticism: Context, Method, and the Book of Jonah.* Minneapolis: Fortress, 1994.

Tuttle, Diane Hoekstra and Dewey G. Cornell. "Maternal Labeling of Gifted Children: Effects on the Sibling Relationship." *Exceptional Children* 59 (1993): 402-10.

Vargon, Shmuel. "The Blind and the Lame." *Vetus Testamentum* 46 (1996): 498-514.

Wender, Paul H. *Attention-Deficit Hyperactivity Disorder in Adults.* New York: Oxford University Press, 1995.

Wertlieb, Ellen C. "Attitudes Towards Disabilities as Found in the Talmud." *Journal of Psychology and Judaism* 12 (1988): 192-214.

Whitman, Barbara Y. and Pasquale J. Accardo. *When a Parent is Mentally Retarded.* Baltimore:Brookes, 1990.

Zornberg, Avivah. "The Concealed Alternative." *Reading Ruth.* Eds. Judith A. Kates and Gail Twersky Reimer. New York: Ballantine, 1994. 65-81.

About the author

Dr. Ora Horn Prouser is executive vice president and dean at The Academy for Jewish Religion. She received her Ph.D in Bible from The Jewish Theological Seminary and has been teaching Bible on the graduate level for over twenty-five years. She has also enjoyed consulting on educational efforts such as the MaToK Bible curriculum and the Day School Standards and Benchmarks Project in Bible. Dr. Prouser has taught and served as scholar-in-residence at many institutions, including synagogues, adult education programs, and camps. She lives in New York with her husband, Rabbi Joseph Prouser, and is the mother of three children.

CPSIA information can be obtained at www.ICGtesting.com
Printed in the USA
LVOW041535261211

260977LV00003B/14/P

9 781934 730355